# The Power of Resurrection

By the Author

*The Wonder of Miracles*
*Anna*

# THE
# POWER
## OF
# RESURRECTION
### BIBLE STORIES THAT LIVE

# MARGARET A.
# GRAHAM

*1817*

Harper & Row, Publishers, San Francisco

Cambridge, Hagerstown, New York, Philadelphia, Washington
London, Mexico City, São Paulo, Singapore, Sydney

FIRST EDITION

---

Library of Congress Cataloging-in-Publication Data

Graham, Margaret A.
  The power of resurrection.

  1. Bible stories, English.   I. Title.
BS550.2.G693  1988    220.9'505    87–45703
ISBN 0-06-063382-4

---

88  89  90  91  92   HC   10  9  8  7  6  5  4  3  2  1

*In Memory of*
*Buddy*
*whom we will see again*

# Contents

# Preface

Writing stories on biblical themes is something different from writing biblical fiction. The difference lies in the perspective. In biblical fiction characterizing individuals, fleshing them out to become full-orbed personalities, is imperative; but in thematic writing emphasis is upon the topic, not the individuals. This does not mean that human interest is lacking; quite the contrary. The reader views events through the mind of an eyewitness—a viewpoint character, if you please—and if the reader is anything like the author, he or she will be intrigued by the background and perception the eyewitness brings to the event.

The reader as well as the author applies imagination to any story. We would both like to think we bring to these stories a "sanctified imagination," which means nothing more than that we do not want to go beyond the boundaries of legitimate exegesis nor get carried away by excesses and miss the truth of what is written.

As a lifelong Bible student and a thirty-year veteran of the classroom (where I taught Bible six hours a day and part of the night and weekends), I thought I knew enough to write these stories. But "getting into the skin" of the eyewitnesses exploded many of my stereotypical concepts, gave me insights I never had before, and stirred my senses with an emotional impact that lingers long after the writing is finished.

In the historical, geographical, and cultural milieu of time and place, understanding is illuminated, and I have gone no farther than any commentator in interpreting events as they are reasonably understood. But the great difference between the story and the sermon is in re-creating that time and place, heightening the sensory drama of the original situation, and bringing into focus the realities as opposed to making extrapolations inherent in the text.

As revelatory as the recreation is, at the same time it raises as many questions as it answers; and the mind is stimulated to probe as far as the Holy Spirit allows into the mysteries of God. Honesty requires the probe, but beyond our comprehension we allow that God should, and indeed does know what we finite creatures cannot know now. And faith teaches that whatever the Spirit withholds from our understanding now, he will eventually reveal in that "great gittin' up mornin'."

> Margaret A. Graham
> Laurinburg, N. C.
> January 1987

# Part I

---

# Old Testament Experiences

# Job

IN MY FLESH I WILL SEE GOD

Scripture Reference: Job 1–3; 12:1–3; 7:20;
9:17, 22; 16:1–14; 19:23–27

J ob was no fool. He was glad that he was financially secure
and his children could live well, but he knew the dangers
of affluence, and he knew what young people could get into.
Drinking wine, they could easily sin and curse God in their
hearts.

He was up early before the sun rose over the rim of the
earth, ordering the servants about. The fieldstones piled high,
the sticks and wood in place, Job had them bring the lamb
which he himself would slaughter before God. Taking off his
mantle, flinging back the sleeves of his cloak, he drew the knife
from his sash and bent over the lamb to examine it.

He had never liked the chore. Butchering a cow did not
bother him, but the lamb was like a child, unsuspecting, trust-
ing. Nevertheless, Job had done it regularly throughout his
adult life.

Its feet bound with cords, the lamb did not struggle as he
laid it on the altar. With his left hand Job held the head down
against a stone and pressed the point of the knife to the throat
until he felt the sharp blade go clean through.

There was not a sound from the lamb as the blood spurted
red against the wool. The body was limp, draped across the
altar like a sack of meal. Job looked across the plain to divert
himself, while the servants skinned and cleaned the lamb.

The Land of Uz stretched out on all sides, its contours

softened by the early light and the dewey haze. So much of it was his. The flocks grazing for miles beyond were all his ... seven thousand at last count and the men who tended them, his servants. He shaded his eyes against the sun and calculated the arrival of his caravans from the east—three thousand camels with silks and spices and whatever else the wool and grain and oil would buy.

The early morning mist was rising from the lake, and a breeze freshened the air. A servant handed him the knife, the blade washed clean, and Job thrust it back in its sheath.

"We'll start the tilling before we shear the sheep," he said as he arranged the wood beneath the sacrifice. "Increase the oxen's feed and water them well." It was no easy job keeping a thousand oxen in shape, maintaining their yokes and harness. With three crops a year to produce the oxen and beasts of burden were kept busy, but it was all very necessary. The abundant harvests supplied the granaries from which the thousands of servants were fed.

Job gazed to the blue hills around the lake and thought of the ancestor for whom the land was named. Did Uz fear God, he wondered. He had heard of a priest of the Most High God named Melchizedec living in Salem, but he had never met him. The man was also King of Salem, he'd heard. *He's probably dead,* Job thought. Sometimes Job felt lonely living among the envious and evil men of Uz. Even his friends were pompous, self-righteous men who loved to talk. The young one, Elihu, was different, inclined to think more than to talk.

But loneliness was not Job's primary concern. He worried about the children. They had never been easy—always tempted by their carnal companions—the oldest boy especially—and now all ten of them were feasting in that son's house. But worry wasn't the answer. He would entreat the Lord for them and God would respect the blood of the sacrificed lamb.

Job took the pot of hot coals from the servant's hands and dumped them onto the wood. Breaking twigs, he covered them and fanned the coals until the twigs burst into flame. Standing back from the crackling fire, Job lifted up his hands and cried out to God, begging forgiveness for his sons and daughters, ". . . lest they sin and curse you in their hearts," he whispered. It gave him great relief, and caused him to praise God.

Job had no way of knowing that something was going on in heaven that vitally concerned him. He could not see into God's presence where the angels of God were presenting themselves for orders. Among them was Satan, that Prince of Darkness who had once, some say, been an angel of light. Conversing with God, Satan was lying as usual, responding to God's inquiry about his activity by saying he'd been strolling up and down in the earth. God, knowing what Satan was about (roaming the earth to victimize anyone he could), asked him, "Have you considered my servant, Job? There is no one on earth like him; he is blameless and upright, a man who fears God and shuns evil."

Well, of course, Satan had considered him. In fact, he champed at the bit to get at Job, but God had put a fence around the man and locked the gates! "Does Job fear God for nothing?" Satan grumbled. "You've fenced him in and blessed him so he's rich. But, if you touch everything he has, he'll curse you to your face!"

"Very well, then," God said, "everything he has is in your hands. But on the man himself do not lay a finger."

With diabolical glee Satan worked feverishly, plotting every move against this wealthiest of landowners. Yes, he'd take away everything Job had, but he'd do it by natural and catastrophic means so the unsuspecting man would think it God's doing and blame God, not him.

Also, he decided, he'd make one swift stroke after another, reserving the worst for last—body blows that worked so well with other men.

And so it was done. With precise timing the attacks fell,

one after the other, and the devastating news was sent to Job wave upon wave.

First, a messenger came streaking across the plain on a camel. White-faced and terrified, he was screaming about desert marauders sweeping down on the oxen and asses while they were feeding. The man was hardly coherent—something about killing the keepers with swords—cutting off heads, slashing and ripping them apart—the thieves making off with every ox and ass Job owned. Only the messenger had escaped the massacre!

And while he was still screaming hysterically, another man came running down the road yelling, "Lightning hit us!" The servants made way for him and let him get to Job. Breathlessly, he gasped, "Thunderbolts right and left!" His thin chest heaving he struggled to speak. "All the sheep are killed! All the men—every one of them!" Frantically, he glanced about as if in the throes of a nightmare. "I left bodies strewn all over, charred black, the stench like a battlefield." His voice grew hoarse, his face contorted with grief. "I ran from one to the other trying to hear a heartbeat, feel a pulse. They were all dead." His face was awash with tears. "Vultures," he sobbed, "vultures are already swarming—tearing away flesh from their bones!"

A woman felt his hair and some of it broke off in her hand. "It's singed—yes, I know," he said. "I don't see how I escaped— oh, help me! I've got to lie down."

They were too stunned to speak, servants and master alike. Standing like statues, trying to get their wits about them, they saw yet another messenger coming. The ass he rode was tired, stumbling along with head down. As the rider came closer they recognized him as one of the camel drivers.

Slowly he dismounted, handing the reins to a boy with a nod toward the watering trough. He was a deliberate man who measured his words. "Chaldeans in three bands hit us—overpowered us in half a day." His eyes were rheumy, half-dazed. "They put the drivers to the sword and led the whole caravan away south." Wiping sweat from his face with his forearm he stalled, trying to control his voice. "I played dead . . . That's how I'm here." They made a place for him to sit and he eased himself down. "When they were gone," he continued, "I picked myself up, found this ass braying behind a dune . . . We've been traveling many days."

The servants commenced wailing, throwing dust in the air. Job eased himself down beside the messenger, his head spinning, his heart pounding in his chest. "There's nothing left," he groaned. "How will I tell my wife . . . my children . . ."

A hush fell over the servants, and Job sensed by the direction of their gaze that someone else was coming. Hearing running footsteps, he closed his eyes. The crowd around him was parting to let someone through. Job lifted his head and gasped! Standing before him was Malachi, his oldest son's servant, ashes on his head, sackcloth about his waist. "What is it?" Job croaked, fearing to ask.

Malchi sank to the ground, too exhausted to stand. "Your sons and your daughters were feasting . . . drinking wine . . . in their oldest brother's house." He was breathing hard, gulping the air. "There came up a great wind—like the thunder of an avalanche—a whirlwind out of the desert . . . Snatched the house off the ground. Ripped it apart!" His wild eyes searched Job's face. "They're all dead, sir . . . All your children are dead!" The horror struck with force. "I made sure . . . Searched the rubble . . . found them all. Every one of them is dead, sir. Only I survived . . ." The man broke down, sobbing.

Job moved to get up and they helped him, lifting him by the elbows, an arm around his waist. Slowly freeing himself of them, Job took his mantle in his two hands and trembling from head to toe, tore it apart. Already a servant was at his side with the basin and he put the razor first to his beard, then to his head. The hair was blown away in the wind and when his face and head were bare, the servant took the basin aside and poured the water on the ground.

Job sank to his knees, leaned down on his arms, then lay prostrate on the ground. At last, his voice rasping, he spoke. "Naked I came from my mother's womb, and naked I will depart. The Lord gave, and the Lord has taken away; may the name of the Lord be praised."

*In all this Job did not sin by charging God with wrongdoing.*

Satan would not give up. The next time angels were summoned before God's throne, he was back, answering every question with a lie. He did not consider himself to be a liar. Sarcastic, perhaps. Never mind. He was biding his time, ready with words he would say and the way he'd say them. "Skin for skin! A man will give all he has for his own life," he blurted out. "But stretch out your hand and strike his flesh and bones, and he will surely curse you to your face."

And the Lord God took the challenge. "Very well, then, he is in your hands; but you must spare his life."

*I'll give him boils, that's what I'll do,* Satan determined. *Have sandflies infect him with the most dreaded kind—boils that cover the head so the hair mats with pus; fill his face so full of them his eyes and mouth can barely open! Cover his back and buttocks with boils so painful he can't sit or stand or lie down. As one boil heals, let the itch torment him until he scratches himself to a bloody pulp, the foul stench of him making his wife nauseated. Children will poke their fingers at him, giggle and run away. When he calls his servant he won't come. That high and mighty Job, I'll make him grovel for a cup of water if his fevered tongue can swallow it! Those friends of his, they'll all come and one by one they'll have a go at him, tear down his confidence, destroy his self-respect. He'll break, he'll break. He'll curse God and die!*

Job sat in the ash heap outside the city where broken pottery littered the rubble, and moaned in the misery he bore. *If only she'd go away, but she won't,* he moaned to himself. *She sits*

*off there with her cowl over her face pressing the cloth over her nose,*
*weeping and pitying me.*

"Curse God and die," she nagged. "Curse God and die."

"You are talking like a foolish woman," he told her. "Shall
we accept good from God and not trouble?" Carefully he
rolled on his side, sucking in his breath at the jets of pain
stabbing him. Reaching for a piece of pottery he began scraping himself, flakes of skin falling away, dead as snakehide in the
spring. The blood oozing, he felt the itching less on that arm,
but then the back of his thigh tormented him. He could hear
voices weeping and wailing.

"Here come your friends," she said, but his head was throbbing and he didn't open his eyes. "Eliphaz, Bildad, and Zo-
phar." Her voice was shrill. "Oh, yes, there's Elihu, too."

As they drew nearer their voices fell silent. In a little while
Job felt a shadow fall across his face and knew they were
standing above him, gawking. He could not bear to see their
stark horror, their torn mantles, their disturbed looks. The
three older ones, perhaps they could say something to explain
all this—say something that would comfort him. The sand
stirred, and the rustle of their garments told him they were
moving away. They were settling down, sitting on the mound
above him where they could catch the air and not his scent.

Seven days and seven nights passed. Observing Job's grief
they scarcely slept, ate little, and did not speak.

Job broke the silence, and cursed the day he was born
saying, "May the day of my birth perish, and the night it was
said, 'A boy is born!' "

Ah, yes. That put the fat in the fire. The three opened
up and they had much to say. One after the other of them
rose to pontificate, and three of them said the same thing.
*They're so sure I've sinned,* Job thought, and with his waning
strength he fought tooth and nail. "Doubtless you are the
people, and wisdom will die with you. But I have a mind as

well as you . . ." He told them in no uncertain terms that he had not sinned—that his suffering was not punishment for some gross misconduct, some violation of the moral code. He was an upright man, and to say otherwise would be a lie. But still the older three came back at him, over and over again with the same accusations, phrased differently but the same.

"Miserable comforters are you all," he muttered, his breath foul to his own nostrils. "Will your long-winded speeches never end? What ails you that you keep on arguing?"

Job knew they weren't listening, and their smugness irritated him exceedingly. So weary, so exasperated, he flung caution to the wind and railed out against God, enumerating all the injustices done to him and blaming God. "It is plain to see that God makes no difference between the righteous and the unrighteous. He treats us both alike. And me?" he roared. "Me he has set up like a target! He takes one shot after another. He's become my enemy!"

But Job fell short of cursing God. In fact, he did quite the opposite.

There, on the ash heap, his life ebbing away, Job declared what he knew to be true despite what he considered to be God's treatment of him.

Oh that my words were recorded,
    that they were written on a scroll,
that they were inscribed with an iron tool on lead,
    or engraved in rock forever!
I know that my Redeemer lives,
    and that in the end he will stand upon the earth.
And after my skin has been destroyed,
    yet in my flesh I will see God;
I myself will see him
    with my own eyes—I, and not another.
How my heart yearns within me!"

# Two Boys and a Man Live Again

WHEN THE BODY TOUCHED ELISHA'S BONES, THE MAN
CAME TO LIFE AND STOOD UP ON HIS FEET.

Scripture Reference: 1 Kings 17, 2 Kings 4:8–37; 13:20–21

It was hot and the skin of water was warm from the heat, but Elijah did not slacken his pace. Climbing the rugged Way of the Sea along the foot of the Lebanon range, he was taking advantage of the shade the mountain cast during the morning hours before the sun climbed over the crest. Over his linen undergarment he wore a camel-skin tunic, which trapped the moisture from his body and wet the skin not exposed to air, helping greatly to cool him. Even so, the heat caused a rash around his waist and made him itch. But Elijah's mind was too occupied to notice.

Jezebel! For Elijah, the last straw was the temple the king let her build to Astoreth. With the fury of God Elijah had risked his life, striding into Ahab's presence with the pronouncement that there would be neither rain nor dew until he said so. The look on the King's face was cynical, so cynical he might have laughed had not Elijah turned on his heel and left him sitting there, sipping his wine.

The subsequent days by the brook did not abate the fury Elijah felt. Every day children, *babies* were being slaughtered by the priests of Baal as if they were sacrificial goats—butchered for the goddess, the roll of drums drowning their screams!

He could not stand it! And as he paced about his campfire at night, he cried out to God.

Alone, except for the ravens that brought him food, Elijah had nothing to do but pray and think. The woman, Jezebel, had Ahab around her little finger—telling him what to do and how to do it. How quickly she had taken over—killing every prophet of God she could find and ordaining priests of Baal by the hundreds. And the people of Israel, like dumb sheep, went right along with her, built shrines and altars to Baal on every knoll and hill! The farmers thought Baal could improve fertility of their stock, control the weather, bless their crops—whatever!

*Well, perhaps the drought will open their eyes,* he fumed. Drinking from the brook and bathing himself in it as long as he could before it dwindled to a stagnant puddle here and there, Elijah was puzzled when the word came that he should go to Zarephath. The town was in Phoenicia, the country from which Jezebel came. The cursed people living there fostered faith in Baal and transported the religion all over the coastal Mediterranean, wherever their sea going vessels sailed.

Along the steep sides of the mountains the giant cedars were still green, nourished by the snowmelt from the peaks. Well, there had been no snowfall since the drought began, and when he crossed the Litani River as it fell west through the gorges to the sea, he noted how low the water level had dropped. The unique springs that ran in the cavernous limestone were beginning to fail. Patches of fertile land on the steep slopes were parched and everyone he saw looked hungry.

The Way of the Sea was a toll road, and to avoid encounter with officials Elijah left the road to follow a trail. In that way he would also avoid Tyre, as licentious a city as Sidon.

By the next day he felt he must be near Zarephath. Hearing the sound of a woodchopper's axe, he followed it until he found the woodcutter and asked if he was near the town.

"Yes," the man replied, "it's below Sidon. There's a short-cut over that ridge. If you'll take the trail here—" and he pointed.

As Elijah made his way up the path he could feel the woodcutter's eyes following him. Perhaps he'd never seen a prophet of God before. Not that a flowing beard was uncommon nor the look of a desert man's skin, but the camel-hair garment, the mantle, that distinguished him.

Elijah wiped his brow, took the last swallow from the skin, and was glad he had not been sent to Sidon. Of course, he understood the city was ideally situated with a harbor that lay like a pool and breezes full of salt. But with Ethbaal, Jezebel's father, king of Sidon, the city was full of vice. Ethbaal served as priest as well as king. And in the worship of Baal he espoused lascivious rites, self-torture, human sacrifice—the kissing of images.

*Strange, the ways of God,* Elijah thought, and wondered again why he was being sent to a heathen woman in Zarephath. Were there no widows in Israel he might help?

Elijah admired the great trees spreading their strong limbs over his head, their trunks reaching for the sky. *No wonder the Phoenicians have such ships—with masts like these!* But the cedars were all he admired about Phoenicia. What Jezebel had done in his beloved Israel made him hate her and all she represented, with perfect hatred.

Elijah thought bitterly upon what had so easily blinded Israel and led her into such debauchery. The floodgates had been opened by Ahab's father, Omri, who arranged the marriage of his son and Jezebel, daughter of the king-priest of Sidon, to effect a political alliance with Phoenicia. Omri, the builder of Samaria, and Ahab, the aficionado of all things Phoenician—art, commerce, religion—were chiefly responsible for Israel's degradation.

Elijah was out of breath, and when he reached the top of the hill he stopped to rest. Gusty wind whipped over the crest, quickly drying the sweat wetting his forearms. Thirst made his lips dry and for a moment he realized how hungry he was. From his vantage he could see the tops of several hills below, and the smoke from the heathen altars rose in the hazy sky like stains against the clear blue. There were no clouds, nor would there be any for some time. Of that he was sure. Perhaps there'd be no clouds until men refused to burn another sacrifice to Baal, and the smoke disappeared again.

Elijah resumed his journey and, coming down the side of the hill, he saw Zarephath strung out along the dusty road, straggling like a tattered cloth scattered by the wind. *Now to find the widow,* he thought.

As soon as he saw a woman picking up sticks, he knew she was the one. Calling out to her, he asked for a drink of water. She was a youngish woman, frail, with eyes set back in her head. She looked at him with a dullness only hopelessness breeds, no energy left for suspicion nor even a curious stare. *Perhaps she recognizes me as a prophet of God,* he thought. With a slight bend of the head she acknowledged his request and turned to oblige. Watching her going away from him, carrying the sticks in her apron, her thin shoulders bowed, he called after her, "And bring me, please, a piece of bread."

The woman stopped. Slowly turning around, she looked at him as if she did not believe what she heard. In a voice so desperate it trembled, she answered, "As surely as the Lord your God lives, I don't have any bread—only a handful of flour in a jar and a little oil in a jug. I am gathering a few sticks to take home and make a meal for myself and my son, that we may eat it—and die."

The plea was for mercy. Was she saying, *Spare me one more day of life?* Elijah did not know. What he did know was that God had sent him to her, and God had told him he would provide flour and oil for her as long as the drought would last.

"Don't be afraid," he told her. "Go home and do as you have said. But first make a small cake of bread for me from what you have and bring it to me, and then make something for yourself and your son. For this is what the Lord, the God of Israel, says: 'The jar of flour will not be used up and the jug of oil will not run dry until the day the Lord gives rain on the land.' "

Briefly, the dull eyes flickered with hope, then narrowed as she considered what he said. Turning again she hesitated, looked back over her shoulder at him, then made her way down the road. Elijah followed her at a distance.

The woman entered one of the houses, and when Elijah reached it he sat down on the step outside. She handed him a gourd of water and he drank it straight down. He could have drunk another but he did not ask. When she went inside he began to look around and there on the step beside him were a man's sandals. A rope tied with a seaman's knot was coiled beside the step. *The widow must have a friend,* he thought.

From inside the house came the soft sounds of the woman moving about making the fire. She was talking quietly with the boy, and from time to time he responded with a moan.

*Now she's mixing the meal and oil in a bowl,* Elijah observed. And in a little while she was slapping the dough, kneading it. He closed his eyes and drifted off to sleep.

The smell of the bread aroused Elijah from his nap, and when he looked up there she was, handing him the pitiful little cake, holding it in both hands as a treasure. Her son leaned against the door, too weak to stand alone, and gazed down at him with the same dull hopelessness of his mother. The boy's belly was distended, the rest of him thin; his arms and legs like sticks. The boy looked like the woman, with the same deep-set eyes and circles.

The taste of the rancid oil made the bread hard to swallow

but, knowing the hunger of the woman and the little boy, he would not spit it out. Elijah wiped his hand across his mouth and studied her as he ate. He wouldn't bother to ask her if there was a man about the place because all she would have to say is, "No" if she were immoral, and if indeed she considered adultery sin. Perhaps the things belonged to her dead husband, he thought, and dismissed the matter from his mind.

Elijah finished the cake and passed the dish to the boy. The child slowly licked the plate, hoping for a crumb. The prophet nodded toward the door, and the woman went inside again. No sooner had she lifted the lid of the flour jar than she gasped. Elijah smiled and climbed the stairs on the outside of the house to the room where he would stay.

Every day thereafter, for weeks and months, the woman baked the little barley cakes and brought them to Elijah. Once the boy was strong enough he sometimes brought the food. The lad was filling out, his limbs getting thicker, his eyes no longer sunk in their sockets. In time he was running about, following the goats on the slopes. In the evenings he would join Elijah under the olive tree or in the prophet's room, but the mother was distant.

At first the woman had marveled at the flour and the oil, the vessels always brimful, but in time she grew accustomed to the full jar and jug, taking the provisions for granted.

One day her son had a fever. She treated him with the usual herbs and was not unduly alarmed, believing he would be better the next day. But that night the lad had a convulsion, then another, one right after the other. Elijah helped her as she frantically bathed him, and tried to spoon the medicine into his mouth.

In a few hours, exhausted by the spasms, the boy lay limp and listless on his mat. Gathering him up in her arms the mother rocked him back and forth, weeping and crying out to any god who would heal her son.

But the boy grew worse and worse until, just before daybreak, his head went back and his open eyes stared unseeing. He did not breathe again!

Grief-stricken, the woman screamed at Elijah, "What do you have against me, man of God? Did you come to remind me of my sin and kill my son?"

Elijah did not answer. Examining the white-lipped child he said, "Give me your son."

Taking the boy in his arms the prophet carried him up to his room. Laying him on his sleeping mat Elijah cried out to the Lord, "O Lord my God, have you brought tragedy also upon this widow I am staying with, by causing her son to die?"

In desperation Elijah then stretched himself over the lifeless form of the boy and prayed, "O Lord my God, let this boy's life return to him!"

Nothing happened. The prophet stood up, paced about the room, tried again. "O Lord my God, let this boy's life return to him!"

The man of God studied the boy, looking for some sign of life. He felt of his face. Cold as ice. He pressed his fingers to the child's throat but could not find a pulse.

Kneeling by the bedside Elijah, deep in thought, stroked his beard. Knowing in his heart of hearts that he must pray again, the prophet took a deep breath, stretched himself over the boy's body for the third time and whispered coarsely, "O Lord my God, let this boy's life return to him!"

Even as he stood up Elijah sensed an answer had been given. A smile crept over him as he watched the blush of life spread up the child's neck, steal into his cheeks! Not waiting for more, he scooped the boy up in his arms and, rushing down the steps, burst in upon the woman. "Look, your son is alive!"

Astonished, her lips parted, afraid to believe. The boy rubbed his nose, looked about as if to say, "Where am I?" and the woman reached for him, trembling with joy! Tears streaming down her face, she looked over her son's head to Elijah and, finding her voice, earnestly whispered, "Now I know that you are a man of God and that the word of the Lord from your mouth is the truth."

The prophet's work in Phoenicia was done, and the next morning he departed for Israel.

But there is another case of a prophet and a boy—similar, but not the same. The prophet was Elisha, successor to the older Elijah. Elisha was an itinerant prophet who traveled from place to place, teaching and working miracles. One of the places he visited regularly was Shunem.

Shunem was a quiet village near Jezreel. It lay opposite Mount Gilboa, as if intimidated by the city of Jezebel's summer palace and the mountain made famous by the Philistine battle in which King Saul's sons were killed and the wounded Saul committed suicide. Elisha included Shunem on his rounds, never intimidated by the wicked Jezebel nor Israel's past military disgraces. Had not Elijah predicted that Jezebel would die by the wall of Jezreel? It would come to pass; it was only a matter of time.

Already the tide had turned against Jezebel. It began when Elijah challenged the prophets of Baal to a contest. All Israel gathered on Mount Carmel to witness the event that would decide which god was the true God. Each side built an altar and prepared a sacrifice, then called on their god to send down fire from heaven to light the sacrifice. The god who answered by fire would be declared the only God. Baal did not answer the prayers of his devotees but God answered Elijah with fire, proving to all Israel that he was the true God. Four hundred and fifty prophets of Baal were slain in reprisal, never again to slaughter babies in sacrifice to Baal, and many Israelites swore allegiance to the God of their fathers.

As furious as she was, Jezebel was never able to recover her losses at Mr. Carmel. Widowed since the death of Ahab in a battle at Ramoth-gilead, the only prospect awaiting Jezebel was her own predicted fate.

Jezebel's son ascended the throne without the political strength to restore Baalism. Instead he sought the gods of Philistia, but soon died and was succeeded by his brother, Jehoram. Jezebel saw herself further stripped of power as Jehoram set about to destroy every vestige of the state religion of Baal and set up another, the worship of golden calves.

The political and religious climate for the prophet Elisha was far from ideal, but it was much improved from the time of Elijah. For instance, in the town of Shunem was a wealthy woman who, like others in Israel, admired the prophet and believed in the one true God. One day she urged Elisha to have a meal with her and her husband. After that, whenever he came to Shunem the woman couldn't do enough for him.

Elisha was a busy man traveling from Bethel to Jericho, to Gilgal, to Shunem and about. From time to time he had dealings with high government officials. Recently there had been the matter of the Moabites, when Jehoshaphat called on the prophet to intervene and save a coalition from a military disaster.

In the circuit of towns Elisha visited there were colonies of young men, student prophets whom he instructed. They were called "sons of the prophet." Always there were personal matters among them, harassments from unbelievers, all sorts of pressing needs.

Elisha had many things on his mind as he rode with his servant Gehazi along the way. It would be good to get to Shunem, particularly now that a freezing rain was pelting down. The donkey he rode didn't seem to mind the cold but he was slow gaited, which made them fall behind Gehazi. At least in Shunem there'd be the warmest kind of hospitality and shelter for as long as they wished to stay.

They rode into town, Elisha shielding himself against the sleet with the same mantle Elijah had worn. So intent was he on protecting his poor bald head, he did not immediately see the addition atop the house. Gehazi dismounted and, taking the reins of Elisha's donkey, waited for the prophet to slide down. Then he led the two animals to the lean-to beside the house where another donkey, a red one, was nuzzling hay. Already the woman had burst out the door and, huddled beneath a shawl, was motioning toward the new steps that led onto the roof. Elisha looked up and blinked. Shielding his face with the mantle, he followed her up the stairs.

Atop the roof was a newly built room. The woman opened the door and stood aside for him to enter. Eagerly, she motioned him inside as Gehazi, carrying their saddlebags, came carefully up the icy steps.

"This chamber is for you," she announced. "My husband and I had it specially built for you and we want you to stay here whenever you come to Shunem." Whether it was pride or grace in her beaming face, he could not tell; he only knew that gladness spread within him like a warming wine. A bed, a table, a stool, and a candlestick—everything he needed for comfort. How gracious she was. He turned to her, trying to think of some way to show his gratitude.

"You need to get out of those wet clothes," the woman told him, and handed him a linen towel. Moving past them, she left the pair alone, closing the door behind her.

Gehazi unpacked the bags with their change of clothing, and when Elisha had toweled himself dry he put on the dry clothes and lay down on the bed. The rattling sleet was lessening outside but the damp cold was penetrating. Pulling up the covers, he covered his head and studied on what he might do for the woman and her husband.

*They have everything,* he thought. *Everything money can buy. Perhaps they'd like a government appointment—some kind of military rank. I could speak to Jehoram or the commander in their behalf.* "Call the Shunammite," he told Gehazi.

The sleet had stopped altogether when Gehazi opened the door, and a pale sun cast light inside the room. Elisha waited for his servant to get down the stairs and then, in the house below, he heard Gehazi's voice and the voice of the Shunammite.

In a few minutes he heard them coming up the steps again. The woman stood at the door as Gehazi ducked his head and came inside. "Tell her this," Elisha told his servant. " 'You have gone to all this trouble for us. Now what can be done for you? Can we speak on your behalf to the king or the commander of the army?' "

Gehazi repeated the message to the woman and Elisha heard her reply. "I have a home among my own people."

*Well,* thought Elisha, *I can understand that.* No doubt they'd lived in Shunem all their lives on ancestral land inherited from their fathers of the tribe of Issachar. There was no reason why they would want to move to Samaria or some military outpost away from family and friends.

The woman dismissed herself, and Gehazi watched her down the steps, then closed the door and sat down on the stool. "What can be done for her?" Elisha asked.

"Well . . ." Gehazi stood up and walked to the window. "She has no son and her husband is old."

Elisha thought upon the matter for a while, then he said, "Call her." While Gehazi fetched the woman again Elisha got up and waited.

When the two of them came back up the stairs the Shunammite paused in the doorway. There was a puzzled expression on her face, as if the matter had been settled and there was nothing more to be said. Elisha smiled at her, and without further ado told her, "About this time next year, you will hold a son in your arms."

Her face turned pale. "No, my lord. Don't mislead your servant, O man of God!"

Elisha smiled. The woman was thinking it was too good to be true. He nodded convincingly and the Shunammite, too excited to speak, hurried down the steps to find her husband.

Just as Elisha had told her, the Shunammite woman bore a son. The old father and the mother were beside themselves with joy, marveling at the gift God had given. Upon arriving in Shunem Elisha and his servant could scarcely get in the house before the happy parents were excitedly telling them the latest development, the latest cleverness of their son. Over the years, as the child grew, he was a pleasure to them all.

Then tragedy struck. A windstorm was coming out of the desert, and with ripened grain standing in the fields, the time was ideal for harvesting. Blasts of hot wind greatly facilitated the threshing, but all hands had to work at breakneck speed to take advantage of it. Men and women were racing about, reaping the last of the grain, unbinding the sheaves, swinging the winnowing forks high in the air as the wind came sweeping out of the east.

The boy was too young to be held responsible, although he had often been told to wear his turban when he went outside. Slipping out of the house bareheaded, he followed his father out in the field where he could romp and play with other children. So busy was the old father, he did not notice the boy except to call to him to ask where his mother was. Running about, jumping in the piles of grain, laughing and playing, the boy grew hot. Unaware of the danger, he did not slow down or seek the shade, and suddenly he keeled over in a faint.

Someone called his father. Seeing the boy pale and unconscious, lying on the ground, he surmised the heat had overcome him. Motioning to a servant he told him, "Carry him to his mother."

The servant promptly obeyed and, with the child in his arms, ran to the house. He turned the boy over to his mother and went back to the field. Seeing her son's condition, his skin hot and dry, the Shunammite held him on her lap, sponging him with cool water, thinking he would soon revive.

The sun rose higher, blistering hot. The mother fanned the boy, kept changing the wet cloth on his forehead, but he did not rouse.

When the sun reached its zenith, the temperature rose higher; the boy's breathing was so shallow it was imperceptible. Fearing for his life the mother thought to put him in a tub of water, but just as she did the boy's eyes rolled back in his head and his mouth fell slack.

Panic stricken, she could not think; and sobbing, she hugged the dead child, rocking back and forth. The little body grew cold in her arms. Then something came over her and she stopped weeping. Getting up, she carried the body outside, and fighting the ferocious wind went up the stairs. Taking her son inside the prophet's chamber, she laid him on Elisha's bed.

Coming back down the steps, the Shunammite ran to the edge of the field, and cupping her hands to her mouth, shouted to her husband. "Please send me one of the servants and a donkey so I can go to the man of God quickly and return."

"Why go to him today?" he yelled back. "It's not the New Moon or the Sabbath."

"It's all right," she answered without explaining.

Soon a servant came across the field with the red donkey in tow. The woman ran to the lean-to and fetched the saddle blanket. *The prophet should be on Mt. Carmel today,* she thought, as she swung the blanket on the animal's back. The servant wanted to oblige her, but she had no time to waste on his slowness.

When the ass was saddled the Shunammite mounted and handed the servant the whip. He would run behind her and goad the donkey forward. "Lead on; don't slow down for me unless I tell you," she told him.

The sun had lowered a bit but it was still high in the sky, and the heat of it and the wind blowing hot as a furnace made the journey torturous; but she was too caught up in her own thoughts to mind. The rocky trail twisted and turned as it made its way up the steep incline, and the servant, sensing the urgency of her mission, drove the donkey mercilessly.

Elisha, atop the mountain near the place of Elijah's altar, looked down and saw the two figures and the donkey. Pointing, he told Gehazi, "Look! There's the Shunammite! Run to meet her and ask her, 'Are you all right? Is your husband all right? Is the child all right?'"

It worried him that the woman was coming. No offering was due—no New Moon or Sabbath observance. It was not like her to bother him with trivial matters. Something must have happened.

Gehazi was running down the trail, slipping and sliding as he went, hampered by the long garment he had not girded up. As he reached the woman Elisha watched closely for any sign that might tell him her trouble. She was pushing Gehazi aside, anxious to continue up the mountain. Gehazi glanced up at him and Elisha motioned him to return. Gehazi hurried up the trail ahead of the woman.

When he reached the prophet Gehazi breathlessly reported, "She said everything is all right."

*Well,* Elisha thought, *that can't be.*

She was coming nearer now, her servant leading the donkey to keep it from stumbling. At first sight of the prophet, the distraught woman got down from the animal and quickly came on foot the rest of the way. Distress showed in her face, and when she reached Elisha she fell on the ground at his feet.

The prophet, seeing her anguish, was greatly perplexed.

*God has hidden her distress from me,* he thought, *and has not told me why.*

Then the woman spoke. "Did I ask you for a son, my lord?" The accusation in the woman's voice stabbed him like a knife. "Didn't I tell you, 'Don't raise my hopes'?"

*So! It is her son.* He turned to Gehazi. "Tuck your cloak into your belt, take my staff in your hand and run. If you meet anyone, do not greet him, and if anyone greets you, do not answer. Lay my staff on the boy's face."

*That should take care of it,* he thought. The case was urgent—no time for dilly-dallying. But when he turned his attention to the woman, she was not satisfied that he had sent his servant. "As surely as the Lord lives and as you live, I will not leave you," she swore.

So, he got up and followed her down the mountain.

They were nearly onto the plain when they saw Gehazi in the distance, returning. Elisha could tell by the way he was walking that he had failed—so sure that when they met Elisha thought to wave him aside with his hand. Instead he listened. "The boy has not awakened," Gehazi told them, and the woman looked at Elisha as if to say, "I told you so."

Elisha began running. When they reached the house he rushed up the steps, went into the room, and saw the boy lying dead on his bed. Shutting the door on the two of them, Elisha knelt down and prayed to the Lord. Remembering what Elijah had done with the boy he raised from the dead, Elisha got up and lay upon the child, his mouth on the boy's mouth, eyes to eyes, hands to hands. He lay there until the small body began to grow warm.

Getting up, the prophet walked to and fro in the room. After a while he stretched himself again over the boy's body. The child began sneezing! As Elisha watched the boy opened his eyes! The prophet went to the door, opened it, and called to Gehazi, "Call the Shunammite."

The servant responded quickly, and the woman came running up the steps. "Take your son," Elisha told her.

She came inside, took one look at the boy, then fell at Elisha's feet, bowing to the floor in gratitude.

Restoring the lad to life was indeed something to be thankful for, and Elisha considered himself fortunate to live at a time when God saw fit to work spectacular miracles. Not since the time of Moses, Joshua, and the Judges had there been such works as those God did through Elijah and now through him. The patriarchs had angelic visitations, he recalled, but never miracles such as these. And Moses, given the miraculous plagues, food and water in the wilderness, and a pillar of fire, never brought the dead back to life. *Since the beginning of the monarchy,* he thought, *there have been no sensational wonders until our time.*

*Solomon, in all his splendor, never knew a single miracle,* the prophet mused. And, David, the man after God's own heart, knew deliverances from his enemies but never by the sun standing still or hailstones killing the enemy.

He thought about the wonderful answers to prayer that always blessed the people of God, but the raising of the dead was unknown to them. He considered that such rare miracles seem to come only when days are the darkest, when most men need their attention called to the power of God. *Yet,* Elisha wondered, *will these spectacular mercies turn Israel back to God and save the country from judgment? If the translation of Elijah did not convince them of God's power, nothing ever will.* Elisha would never forget the awesome sight of Elijah being caught up to heaven; yet, looking at the Shunammite mother reunited with her child—kneeling by the bedside, kissing her son, stroking his hair—he thought that nothing quite surpassed that.

Elisha never raised another person to life, but a strange and mysterious resurrection is directly associated with him. After a prophetic ministry spanning fifty-five years, Elisha became

ill and died. He was buried, perhaps somewhere in the valley
of the Jordan.

In the spring of the year, when bands of Moabite raiders
often slipped over the border and attacked Israelites, some men
of Israel were tending to the burial of a man. Suddenly they
saw a band of Moabites! If they wanted to escape with their
lives, they had to make quick work of the burial and flee.
Seeing a tomb nearby, they quickly decided to dump the
corpse into it and run.

Throwing the body on top of the skeleton already inside
the tomb, they were shocked to see the corpse of their friend
come alive! As soon as the dead body touched Elisha's bones,
life was restored to the man and he stood up on his feet.

# Part II

---

# Old Testament Writings

# 3

# David

WHEN I AWAKE, I WILL BE SATISFIED . . .

Scripture Reference: 1 Samuel 23; Psalm 16, 17, 73;

Job 19:23–27; 14:14, 15; Genesis 22

Lying on his back, his arm across his eyes, David tried to shut out the sounds of men milling about, filing their swords, scraping their shields. Bone tired, he needed sleep; but the men were restless, disgruntled ever since they left Keilah. Naturally, they wanted to stand up and fight the enemy and hated this retreating, always retreating. *As if I don't hate it, too,* David said to himself, *but there's no other way. Saul is God's anointed; we dare not touch him lest we violate all that's holy.*

Intermittently dozing, he could hear the men grumbling and he understood their discontent. As the chase went on, day in and day out, the only tactic he commanded was dodging, confusing the enemy, and that was not a fighting man's tactic. Scrambling up cliff sides, hiding in gullies and ravines was a coward's way. As they kept on the run rations were depleted, water scarce, desert heat unbearable.

David still found it hard to believe that the people of Keilah could be so ungrateful, nor could his six hundred troops who had rescued the town from the Philistines accept such ingratitude. After such kindness how could the men of Keilah turn around and betray David and his men to Saul, tell him their whereabouts! Fortunately, God had warned David and they got away. *Good thing I asked,* David thought.

He rolled over on his side and gazed at the rugged terrain before him. *No wonder they call this mountain "gloomy,"* he thought. The bare ochre-colored earth of Hachilah lay baking in the sun as it had for a thousand years. Hebron, to the northwest, was better situated. It was lush with vineyards on every slope of the Valley of Eschol.

*How long will this go on?* he wondered. *Jonathan seems to think it won't be long.* David smiled as he thought of Jonathan. What a friend! Risking his life, he had sneaked out of his father's camp to come to David in the woods. *He knew I'd be discouraged, depressed, and he came to give me the words I needed to bear.*

Commotion interrupted his thoughts. Raising his head, he saw soldiers crowding around one of the scouts coming toward him. Getting to his feet, David waited.

Hollow-eyed and breathless, the soldier gasped, "They're closing in!"

"Which direction?"

"North, northwest."

"How many?"

"Two thousand . . . maybe more."

"How much time do we have?"

"Less than half a day, sir."

David glanced at the sun. "We might be able to make the Rock of Maon." Quickly signaling his armor bearer, he gave the order to the captain, "Joab, break camp!" Taking the lead, he headed south on the trail.

Despite the scorching sun they dared not slacken their pace, but the unavoidable happened. In a narrow pass a flock of sheep choked the way, and they had to wait their turn. "They belong to Nabal," Joab told him. "Biggest sheep man in the area. We could force them to let us through."

David shook his head, glanced at the sun again. Already it was lowering, riding just above the western hills. "Alert the men. If Saul overtakes us from behind, give the order to keep swords in scabbard, arrows in quivver."

The captain's face hardened.

"Do as I say," David commanded.

Smarting from the order, David turned his attention to the sheep. "Can't you move them faster?" he yelled at the sheep herder, but the man did not hear him.

When at last the passage was cleared, David's troops quickly poured through. Soon they were cautiously skirting the plain where the town of Maon lay.

By the time they were safely past the town the sun was behind the hills, the light fading fast. Gingerly they threaded their way along a ledge to the Rock.

The ordeal left the men limp with exhaustion. Too tired to speak, they sank to the floor of the cavern and ate their dried meat in silence. Lying down to sleep, they seemed piled in heaps like sacks of sand, and in no time at all the sounds of snoring began.

The dank cave was airless, foul with the stench of unwashed bodies, and David could not sleep. Picking his way, stepping over the sleeping forms, he made his way outside.

A hot blast of wind blowing in from the Dead Sea swept the sky of any trace of cloud, leaving the stars strewn across the heavens like so many brilliant diamonds. David took up a position on a promontory where he could look to the north. His eyes roving over the landscape, he searched the mountainside for sight of a campfire—any sign of the enemy. There was no smoke, nothing to see. He thought to lie down outside, but just as he did the sounds of running footsteps alerted him. *What now?* he worried, seeing a scout hurrying to report.

The man's voice was coarse with fear. "They're on the other side of the mountain."

"The other side of this mountain?"

"Yes, the other side."

He had expected an approach from the north.

"Are we trapped, sir?" the runner asked.

David did not answer. Dismissing the man, he went back inside the cavern. *We're trapped, all right,* he thought. *With first light Saul's men will move in from both sides and we'll have no way of escape. We've got to get out of here.* Intending to wake

Joab, he was just about to lay his hand on the captain's shoulder when he paused. Thinking better of it, he went outside again. Lifting his eyes toward the stars, David waited. Then he began speaking softly.

> Hear, O Lord, my righteous plea;
>     listen to my cry.
> Give ear to my prayer—
>     it does not rise from deceitful lips.

The tumult inside him churned, and David's voice was raised, rumbling with the agitation he felt.

> May my vindication come from you;
>     may your eyes see what is right.
> Though you probe my heart and examine me at night,
>     though you test me, you will find nothing;
>     I have resolved that my mouth will not sin.

It was all so unfair—Saul chasing him like some animal for no reason. Indignation welled up in David, causing him to speak harshly.

> As for the deeds of men—
>     by the word of your lips
> I have kept myself
>     from the ways of the violent.
> My steps have held to your paths;
>     my feet have not slipped.

The Holy Spirit began to temper him, reminding him that he would be vindicated. The vehemence subsided, and David felt calmer, his language tender, smoother.

> I call on you, O God, for you will answer me;
>     give ear to me and hear my prayer.

> Show the wonder of your great love,
>    you who save by your right hand
>    those who take refuge in you from their foes.
> Keep me as the apple of your eye;
>    hide me in the shadow of your wings
> from the wicked who assail me,
>    from my mortal enemies who surround me.

The mention of his enemies agitated him again, and his voice tightened.

> They close up their callous hearts,
>    and their mouths speak with arrogance.
> They have tracked me down, they now surround me,
>    with eyes alert, to throw me to the ground.
> They are like a lion hungry for prey,
>    like a great lion crouching in cover.
> Rise up, O Lord, confront them, bring them down;
>    rescue me from the wicked by your sword.
> O Lord, by your hand save me from such men,
>    from men of this world whose reward is in this life.

David was reflecting upon what he had said. Looking up at the stars, the Holy Spirit told him again that the wicked have reward only in this life, whereas he had present and future rewards with God, and he went on with his prayer.

> You still the hunger of those you cherish;
>    their sons have plenty,
>    and they store up wealth for their children.
> And I—in righteousness I will see your face;
>    when I awake, I will be satisfied with seeing your
>    likeness.

His eyes moist, David lingered, savoring the comfort that flooded his soul. Then he turned to go inside and discovered

Joab standing behind him. "Wake the men, Joab. We've no time to lose."

Quickly the soldiers buckled on their swords, gathered up their spears, bows, and shields, and filed out in the night. As they slipped in and out around the rock, desperately trying to escape, they were hardly prepared for the outcome. With the first show of light in the eastern sky they were sure of attack; but, pressing on, they saw no sign of the enemy.

As the sun rose higher they were easy targets, and frantically they scrambled to get out of reach. Suddenly a trumpet sounded. Halting in their tracks they waited for the word to be passed. "Hold up. All's clear," they were told.

Shocked, they asked, "What happened?" and the words of the scouts were related. "Philistines are raiding the country. Saul had to call off the chase to go after the Philistines!"

The troops let out a whoop! Jubilation abounded! Laughing and back-slapping, their high spirits racing, they celebrated with abandon. David slipped away from them, and on his knees thanked God for the deliverance.


When the excitement died down some of the men went looking for a spring in which to bathe; others stretched out in the shade to sleep.

David was standing on a little knoll watching the slow circling flight of buzzards. Joab drew alongside and stood watching with him. In a few minutes Joab broke the silence. "I heard you praying last night."

"Well, he answered didn't he?"

"That he did." Joab hesitated, cleared his throat. "What did you mean when you said, 'When I awake, I will be satisfied with seeing your likeness'?"

"Just that."

"Did you mean you'd be satisfied to live through the night?"

David smiled. "No, not that."

"What then?"

David paused. "I meant, if I should die, I will be satisfied with seeing God."

Joab groped awkwardly for words, hesitating to ask. "You're sure about that?"

"You mean about seeing God after I die?"

Joab nodded, his face grimey from the sweat and dirt.

"As sure as Job."

"Job?"

"Yes, Job. He was so sure he'd see God, so confident, he wanted his words engraved with an iron tool and lead, or engraved in a rock forever."

"What words?"

"His words about life after death, about a living Redeemer, about the resurrection of his body . . . Job believed he would see his Redeemer with his own eyes even if his body had moldered in the grave."

"Job said all that?"

"He did." David reached for a piece of straw. "And more than that. You know, Job was a man who asked questions and got answers."

"What kind of questions?"

"Well, for instance, he once asked, 'If a man dies, will he live again?' "

"So?"

"Well, he had the answer. He said, if I remember correctly, 'All the days of my hard service I will wait for my renewal to come. You will call and I will answer you; you will long for the creature your hands have made.' "

" 'Renewal?' "

" 'Release,' something like that."

"From the grave?"

"From the grave."

Joab shook his head disdainfully. "I don't understand how he knew all that . . . There isn't much even in the Torah about life after death . . . I wonder why?"

"You shouldn't wonder about that. Look around you. There isn't a religion in the world that doesn't have grandiose myths about what happens to a man once he dies. Egyptians, Babylonians, you name it, they all have weird, abominable beliefs about death and life beyond the grave. We Hebrews know what we believe about immortality and resurrection, but we'd cause all kinds of confusion if we went beyond a simple statement here and there."

The buzzards tilted the tips of their wings gliding on an upsurge of the hot wind.

The men walked over to the shade of the cliff and sat down, their backs against the stone. David was glad for the opportunity to talk about a subject that keenly interested him. "I believe Abraham was thinking about resurrection when he laid the knife to Isaac's throat."

"You do? What makes you think that?"

Looking out across the valley, David picked his teeth with the straw. "Well, Abraham knew the promise God had made, that all the families of the earth would be blessed through his descendants; and since God had rejected Ishmael, Isaac was his only son. If Isaac was sacrificed, God would have to raise him from the dead, otherwise the promises could not be kept."

"That makes sense." Joab unbuckled his girdle and laid his sword beside him. "I always wondered why God made Abraham and Isaac travel three days to Mount Moriah—"

"You mean Zion where Jerusalem stands?"

"Yes, Zion."

David shook his head. "That's always puzzled me, too . . . And, the ram caught in the thicket just as Abraham had said. Remember he said, 'God will provide a lamb for the burnt offering'?"

"How'd he know that, David?"

"We've always known a sacrifice will be given, a Redeemer such as Job talked about. The lambs, the rams—there'll be an end to them some day. God will provide a sacrifice."

Several soldiers were coming into view at the bottom of the hill and were hollering up to them. Joab caught the gist of what they were yelling. "They've found a spring to swim in."

David got to his feet. "Good! Let's go."

Years later, when David had survived all his ordeals with Saul and become king over all Israel, he planned the dedication of his palace on Mt. Zion. Many things had happened in his public and private life which made the dedication of the citadel important. Absalom's rebellion had caused David great suffering, and after the defilement of David's concubines on the roof of his palace, reconsecration was in order.

The dedication had been delayed because David lay ill, his life in jeopardy. As he picked up the lute that morning, strummed it, tuned the strings, he was glad to be alive. Recovery had been slow and painful, but it was all behind him now. He felt strong enough, but he would never be vigorous again.

Spreading a scroll of papyrus on the table before him, he weighted down the ends with flat sticks then opened the vial of ink and reached for the camel-hair brush. Quietly the Holy Spirit was prompting words to the music he was humming. He stopped humming and sighed.

> Keep me safe, O God,
>   for in you I take refuge.
> I said to the Lord, 'You are my Lord;
>   apart from you I have no good thing.'

He wrote it all down just as it came to him, reread it, then closed his eyes. Strumming the lute he sang the words to the melody.

Love God he did, but David also wanted to express his love for the people of God. He tried two lines, the words did not work; and then he wrote:

As for the saints who are in the land,
  they are the glorious ones in whom is all my delight.

That satisfied him. But the Spirit was directing him away
from the saints to the idols of the heathen, the gods of Moab,
Edom, Damascus. He thought of people he knew, Israelites
who had turned their backs on God and followed the folly of
idolatry. Bloodstained from offerings, they were abominable;
the judgment of God inevitable.

The sorrows of those will increase
  who run after other gods.
I will not pour out their libations of blood
  or take up their names on my lips.

The words were sufficient. The Holy Spirit gave him no
more about idolatry. He got up and dipped a gourd in the
crock for a drink of milk.

As he drank, he considered again God's faithfulness in
restoring the stability of his government and his house. He
thought about the extended boundaries of his kingdom—hard
fought, but won.

Lord, you have assigned me my portion and my cup;
  you have made my lot secure.
The boundary lines have fallen for me in pleasant places;
  surely I have a delightful inheritance.
I will praise the Lord, who counsels me;
  even at night my heart instructs me.
I have set the Lord always before me.
  Because he is at my right hand,
  I will not be shaken.

The brush in his hand trembled. The sickness was past but
age was coming on; the tremble, the dark brown spots on the
backs of his hands told him that. David rubbed his forearm

thoughtfully. Once the flesh had been muscle, now the forearm must be flexed to show any muscle at all. Through the open doorway he could see the misty valley below, and he thought of where they would bury him on the mountain. He shrugged his shoulders. *What does it matter?* he thought, and reached again for the brush.

> Therefore my heart is glad and my tongue rejoices;
>     my body also will rest secure,
> because you will not abandon me to the grave,
>     nor will you let your Holy One see decay.
> You have made known to me the path of life;
>     you will fill me with joy in your presence,
>     with eternal pleasures at your right hand.

David wiped the brush, sealed the vial of ink, and reread the psalm. When he was finished he leaned back, his hands folded behind his head; looking up at the ceiling he realized his eyes were brimming with tears.

Outside his window David caught the strains of people singing; going to the door he could hear the tune, one of Asaph's songs sung by pilgrims. He remembered how Asaph struggled with the problem in that song—the problem of the righteous suffering and the wicked prospering. David smiled as he thought of it. In his youth he, too, had wondered why the righteous do not always succeed nor the wicked always fail. The opposite seemed often to be the case.

But the Holy Spirit resolved poor Asaph's puzzlement— showed him that this life must always be viewed in light of life which is to come. The pilgrims were rounding the last curve in the road, singing:

> Yet I am always with you;
>     you hold me by my right hand.
> You guide me with your counsel,
>     and afterward you will take me into glory.

Whom have I in heaven but you?
And being with you, I desire nothing on earth.
My flesh and my heart may fail,
but God is the strength of my heart
and my portion forever.

*Ah, Asaph had the answer,* David mused. *The righteous have God now and they will have him forever. What greater portion could be given?*

David was about to turn away from the door when he realized something was rubbing up against his leg. He looked down to see a little yellow kitten on unsteady legs looking up at him, its round eyes pleading, its weak voice meowing. David reached down and lifted the kitten up in his arm. "Come, I'll give you some milk," he said, and lifting the lid of the crock, he scooped up a gourdful.

# 4

# Ezekiel

CAN THESE BONES LIVE?

Scripture Reference: Ezekiel 37; Isaiah 26:19; Psalm 17:15

Ezekiel often thought of the past, of his home in Jerusalem near the Temple. Being brought to Babylon when he was twenty-five, he had settled near Nippur along the Chebar with other Jews, and within five years God summoned him to prophesy. Within another five years, on the day the final seige of Jerusalem began, Ezekiel's young wife died; and, though his heart was heavy as stone, he was told not to mourn publicly. The message was clear: The nation Judah was going to die; and because her judgment was so well-deserved, mourning would be inappropriate.

The captives already in Babylon were not oppressed; they had freedom to buy and sell, build houses, establish businesses. The Chebar, an irrigation canal connecting the Tigris and Euphrates, bordered by branch willows and lush green fields, made a pleasant place to live and work. Other Jews who settled in the north, far from the wicked capital, enjoyed freedom from idolatrous excesses. Every passing year the exiles became more content, satisfied that some of their own people ranked high in the government.

But with the fall of Jerusalem imminent and some of the last of the deportees brought to live along the Chebar, Ezekiel could not escape the anguish the older Jews expressed every day in a thousand ways. They never sang, and at the slightest provocation they wept. They grieved that they would never see their homeland again, and Ezekiel was inclined to think he, too, would never see it again.

There was little time, however, for Ezekiel to speculate about his own fate, so taken up was he with the ecstatic revelations God was giving him. Poor Jeremiah, whom he had known briefly in his youth, was so occupied with the devastation little comfort was given him; but Ezekiel enjoyed visions of the future in which there were at least mixed blessings. Like Daniel, who lived in the Babylonian court, Ezekiel's revelations were apocalyptic, electrifying visions.

The Jews did not take kindly to Ezekiel's preaching, his unconventional methods, his symbols, images, and allegories. He used parables, proverbs, and language they found difficult to comprehend. Nor did they understand his revelations. They wanted something for their present condition, and Ezekiel seemed only given to purging them of their idolatry. They complained that their nation was dying and would never live again. What, then, of the promises of God? The covenant made with Abraham?

Ezekiel did not remember the day nor the hour when God revealed to him the answer to their question. The Holy Spirit took charge of him, carried him about at will, showing him a vast area littered with human bones. Ezekiel saw disjointed skeletons—spinal columns, the rib cages intact; domes of skulls, jawbones with teeth, eye sockets filled with sand; finger bones, rings encircling them; shinbones and hipbones, all scattered about as if slung here and there, washed by wind and rain, bleached by desert sun.

Walking back and forth he saw some bones broken, some deformed, all dry as dust; fragile, so porous that if they were held up to the sun the light would shine through. Then God asked him, "Son of man, can these bones live?"

"O Sovereign Lord, you alone know."

"Prophesy to these bones and say to them, 'Dry bones, hear the word of the Lord! This is what the Sovereign Lord says to these bones: I will make breath enter you, and you will come to life. I will attach tendons to you and make flesh come upon you and cover you with skin; I will put breath in you, and you will come to life. Then you will know that I am the Lord.' "

Ezekiel, trembling, spoke, telling the bones what God had told him to say, and as he was speaking he heard noises—a rattling sound—for the bones were coming together! Spinal columns joined hipbones and skulls; arm and leg bones fitted into sockets; foot bones and hand bones joined wrists and ankles, and there, before his astonished eyes, tendons formed and flesh with skin covered them! Lying on the ground were thousands of bodies, dead but recreated!

God spoke to him again. "Prophesy to the breath; prophesy, son of man, and say to it, 'This is what the Sovereign Lord says: Come from the four winds, O breath, and breathe into these slain, that they may live.' "

Ezekiel, still shaking, obeyed. Before his very eyes the corpses began breathing, opened their eyes, looked around, and began getting to their feet! Single files formed, and soon, standing row on row was a formidable army!

Then Ezekiel heard God say, "Son of man, these bones are the whole house of Israel. They say, 'Our bones are dried up and our hope is gone; we are cut off.' Therefore prophesy and say to them: 'This is what the Sovereign Lord says: O my people, I am going to open your graves and bring you up from them; I will bring you back to the land of Israel. Then you, my people, will know that I am the Lord, when I open your graves and bring you up from them. I will put my Spirit in you and you will live, and I will settle you in your own land. Then you will know that I the Lord have spoken, and I have done it, declares the Lord."

The vision quickly faded; God's voice fell silent. Ezekiel sat staring out over the plain with unseeing eyes. Weak as water, he did not try to stand. As if in a trance, only slowly did he return to the realities of his surroundings. As he did he felt aroused, excitement infusing him with zeal to tell the good news. But he knew the Jews. *How can I make them believe?* he wondered. *They'll ask how long they must wait . . . Seventy years? They'll laugh in my face.*

Knowing he would need all the reinforcement he could get, Ezekiel tried to remember if any of the other prophets had been given a similar message. The song of Isaiah came to mind:

> But your dead will live;
> their bodies will rise.
> You who dwell in the dust,
> wake up and shout for joy.
> Your dew is like the dew of the morning;
> the earth will give birth to her dead.

*Did Isaiah mean the restoration of Israel,* Ezekiel asked himself, *or did he mean the bodily resurrection of individuals?* He could not decide. The words sounded much like David's faith in personal immortality:

> And I—in righteousness I will see your face;
> when I awake, I will be satisfied with seeing your
> likeness.

*Even so, if one person can be raised, why not a nation?* Ezekiel reasoned. *If only I can convince them that God will raise our nation again—*

Ezekiel turned his back to the sun for the warmth it would give him, closed his eyes, and continued to cogitate. *If only I can make them see that it's no more for God to raise a nation than one man . . . make them see there's life after this death for the nation Israel.*

He could agonize no longer. Getting up, Ezekiel took the hard-worn path by the canal back to Nippur.

# 5

# Daniel

MULTITUDES WHO SLEEP IN THE DUST WILL AWAKE.

Scripture Reference: Daniel 10–12

Daniel dismissed his Persian driver and, climbing out of the chariot, walked unsteadily to the bank of the river. Not only was he feeble from age, he had been fasting for twenty-one days, mourning the revelation that concerned a great war.

The Tigris was a willful river; flooding, it ruined crops, washed away topsoil, played havoc with the fields. Daniel looked in the direction of the steep Armenian mountains where snowmelt in springtime streamed down, gushing, plunging into the river; but they were too distant and his eyesight too poor to see them. He tried to see across the Tigris to the Shinar Plain, where grain no doubt waved restlessly in the breeze; but his vision was cloudy, all he could see was a haze.

That day the river was peaceful, so shallow a boat was being portaged north. *How easily the Medes and Persians had forded the Tigris when they came to conquer Babylon,* Daniel sighed. *Poor Babylon.*

He sighed again. *Poor Israel,* he thought. *We've been full cycle—Abraham leaving this region at the command of God; his people in the intervening years, twice bondmen, finally now brought back here.* Daniel shook his head. *Now that they're reprieved, allowed to return to the Promised Land, I wonder if they understand what lies ahead for them? . . . If only I were not so old,*

*I would've returned with them. No matter,* he told himself, and turned his attention to the boat being lifted.

With such dim vision he could not make out the markings but, from the cut of the sail, he guessed the vessel was from the Indus. *Too small for timber,* he reasoned; *it must be hauling spices, maybe gold or cloth.*

Flies were bothering him and he slapped at one persisting about his face. *It's the twenty-fourth day of the month,* he told himself, as if marking the time could hasten things. Troubled as he was by the revelation, he thought upon the scriptures. How full they were of judgment, of reward. He considered Job and how his estate was finally settled, the books balanced, if you please. Job's Redeemer would be just and, either in this life or the next, justice would prevail; of that he was sure.

Suddenly he looked up, and there a man stood before him. But this was no ordinary man dressed in linen. His face was like lightning, his eyes like flames, his arms and legs like bronze! When he spoke his voice sounded like a roaring crowd.

What God's messenger said to him struck Daniel dumb, and he bowed himself to the ground. The man reached down and touched his lips and Daniel was able to speak. "How can I, your servant, talk with you, my lord? My strength is gone and I can hardly breathe."

Then the messenger spoke reassuringly and strengthened him. Revived, Daniel slowly sat up and listened as the angel delivered his message. First, the future of Persia was outlined and its defeat by Greece. But there was more—the Grecian Empire would divide into four principalities. After that—!

The vision was as dark as midnight, detailing unprecedented suffering for God's people at the hand of the cruelest of dictators. Then the messenger said, "At that time Michael, the great prince who protects your people, will arise. There will be a time of distress such as has not happened from the beginning of nations until then."

The barrage of words was so rapid Daniel scarce could take them in. Leaning forward he strained to hear what more would be said.

"But at that time your people—everyone whose name is found written in the book—will be delivered. Multitudes who sleep in the dust of the earth will awake: some to everlasting life, others to shame and everlasting contempt. Those who are wise will shine like the brightness of the heavens, and those who lead many to righteousness, like the stars for ever and ever . . ."

Then the angel told Daniel to seal the book "until the time of the end."

For many days Daniel meditated on what the messenger had told him. Carefully recording the words, he felt the message's burden of gloom was relieved by the promise of deliverance, of the righteous dead rising to everlasting life; the unrighteous to everlasting punishment. What cheered him most was the thought that those who led others to righteousness would shine like stars.

He thought of his own influence in Babylon and in the Persian court and the influence of other Hebrews. The wise men of the East had not been able to compete with the wisdom God imparted to men of faith. The outstanding miracles God had performed in their behalf had struck fear and faith in many a heathen heart, and for this Daniel was glad.

He rolled the scroll for the last time, waited for the wax to soften, then sealed the edge seven times. Tired, he closed his eyes and tried to visualize the multitude of the dead in every age and every place, rising from the dust to meet their Maker.

# Part III

---

# Old Testament Ascensions

# 6

# Enoch

GOD TOOK HIM

Scripture Reference: Genesis 5;

Hebrews 11: 5–7; Jude 14, 15

Methuselah was in his nine-hundred-and-sixty-ninth year, having lived longer than every other ancestor.* He had even outlived his own son, Lamech, who died eighty-seven years before. Oh, yes, he remembered dates and events clearly and could recite the family tree eight generations back to Adam.

As he sat by the stream that ran past his place and emptied into the gulf, he mused upon his longevity. Never in his life had he suffered any serious illness. Though he had heard of the pox, he was never its victim nor was he given to simple fevers such as some people had. The world itself was a healthy environment with warm, moist air and an unchanging temperature. Of course, he understood that it was not perfect, that there was once a time and place when briars and thorns did not grow, when animals were not wild.

Nevertheless, Methuselah could not make up his mind if long life was a blessing or a curse. Perhaps it didn't make much difference which side he came down on—according to his grandson, Noah, God was going to destroy them all with a flood. Well, he didn't know what to make of that grandson. Was he going to save the world or go down in history as a lunatic?

---

* The genealogy in Genesis 5 may be considered a record of dynasties rather than individual life spans. If life spans, Methuselah died in the year of the flood; but whether or not he died in the flood is not known.

Methuselah fanned a fly from his brow and looked out over the Sumerian plain. Shipping in the gulf was a thriving business, carrying the grain from the rich delta land to ports where wool and ivory would be exchanged. Still, the ship Noah had built was unlike anything he'd ever seen—no bow, no stern.

Methuselah shook his head thinking how Noah was somewhat like Lamech, his son, Noah's father. Lamech was a melancholy soul, working hard from dawn to dusk, never able to accept the way things were. Methuselah remembered the night Noah was born; Lamech gave the child that name which meant "comfort," and in his solemn way said, "He will comfort us in our labor and painful toil of our hands caused by the ground the Lord has cursed."

Methuselah knew his share of toil, but he had lived long enough to appreciate the great strides people had made. Early on, as his grandfather had told him, Cain's family had domesticated animals, cultivated grain, worked in ore, invented music—even organized village life. Outstanding accomplishments, considering they had no models or precedents to build upon. Of course Cain's people were ungodly, and what the righteous family of Seth had done was not recorded in terms of material progress. They were expected to live their lives in the tradition of their godly ancestors, like his father Enoch, but here of late . . . well, they were intermarrying with the ungodly and the results of those marriages were anything but promising.

Methuselah was secretly proud of his grandson, Noah. It was no small courage that made him speak out against the things that were going on. For a century he'd been decrying the violence and wickedness in the world. *Noah is more like my father than anyone else,* Methuselah mused as he watched a raven circling above the ark. *He's exactly like Enoch; he walks with God.*

The memory of his father had not grown dim in all the long years since his disappearance. Methuselah was three hundred years old when it happened, married and a father himself. All of his life he had observed his father, and the man had never disappointed him. Enoch stood head and shoulders above other men as a man of God, a stickler for doing what was right no matter what the circumstances. *They gave him the right name,* Methuselah thought. *Enoch—"teacher." If ever a man taught by example as well as word, it was my father. Of course, he wasn't perfect, but there wasn't a person who knew him who did not agree that my father Enoch pleased God.*

It was on a morning shortly after dawn that Enoch disappeared. When the alarm went out all the sons and daughters and everyone in the neighborhood responded. There was no evidence anywhere of foul play nor signs of an animal attack. A search party combed the woods and, when Enoch wasn't found, they dragged the lake thinking he might have drowned.

All along, Enoch's wife and children knew in their hearts what had happened. "God took him," they said, and the neighbors were not hard to convince. *That's the kind of man he was,* Methuselah reflected. *Enoch walked with God.*

Methuselah remembered with great clarity the joy and fear he felt at that time. It had never left him. Yet, *why* God had taken his father had never been explained and the question often occupied his mind.

Methuselah looked out across the beautiful grassland where Noah's incredible ship stood completed and ready for the animals he was rounding up. As Methuselah's thoughts roamed about, still seeking an explanation, he drowsed, his eyes half-closed. The distant voices of the workmen, the sounds of their tools, served only as an accompaniment to his weariness. Then, suddenly, a thought occurred to him! His eyes flew open, he sat straight up. *Can it be that God took Enoch to heaven without dying to escape the judgment of a flood?*

Gazing with unseeing eyes, Methuselah let the idea swirl in his head. He thought upon it for some time until weariness overtook him again. He lay back against the tree. *Who knows?* he mumbled.

Gusty wind whipped about, the sound of it waking him. The skies were rumbling with a strange and alarming sound. He got up and went inside.

# 7

# Elijah

ELIJAH WENT UP TO HEAVEN IN A WHIRLWIND.

Scripture Reference: 1 Kings 18–19; 2 Kings 1–2; Matthew 17:1–3

The old prophet was making his last rounds. For years he had traveled between the cities of Israel, visiting the schools of the prophets, teaching them, praying with them. At his side was his protegé, the one God had told him to appoint, a farmer named Elisha.

That last night in Gilgal they talked of many things, but Elijah had his own thoughts as well. After Elisha was asleep the old prophet lay awake going over in his mind the years of service that lay behind him. The power of God had been real in his life—so much so that he was hard put to decide which of the experiences was the greater. For Israel, undoubtedly, the contest with the Baal prophets on Mt. Carmel was the greatest. To this day he could hear the sky split as the fire fell and hear the "whoosh" as water turned to steam! Astonished, the people stood wide-eyed and open-mouthed, seeing the spectacle, smelling the roasting flesh. And when the question was put to them, how quickly they responded: "The Lord, he is God! The Lord, he is God!"

At his challenge Israelites fell upon the Baal prophets and slaughtered them until blood puddled the ground beneath their feet and there was not another head to roll. Gruesome, but fitting justice for the killers of babes.

King Ahab was profoundly impressed by the demonstration; and following on the heels of it was Elijah's announcement that the drought would soon be over. Ahab was greatly relieved to hear that rain was coming and cooperated with everything Elijah told him to do.

Oh, what a rain that was! Sheets of it swept across the mountains and valleys, dry stream beds flooded, roads were overrun, and Elijah, by the Spirit of God, ran ahead of Ahab's chariot all the way to Jezreel.

Ah, yes, Jezreel . . . That episode he would like to forget. Hearing of the slaughter of her prophets, Jezebel swore to take Elijah's life and Elijah fled from Jezreel like a scared rabbit. In the desert, beyond the woman's reach, he sat down under a broom tree and prayed that he might die. "I have had enough, Lord," he said. "Take my life; I am no better than my ancestors."

Exhausted, he lay down under the bush and fell asleep. How long he slept he did not know, but quite suddenly he was awakened by someone touching him. Above him stood an angel, and at his head a jar of water and some hot bread baked over coals. "Get up and eat," the angel said.

He did as he was told. And when he finished the food he washed it down with the water, licked his fingers, and without knowing what happened to the angel, lay back down again.

Elijah was in a deep slumber when the angel touched him a second time. Again he was told, "Get up and eat, for the journey is too much for you."

Obediently he ate, and afterward he felt strong enough to press on. Taking the staff he'd carried for years, he headed southeast for the Sinai range barely visible in the distance. Sand, blown by the hot wind, bombarded him. Leaning into the wind he clutched the flapping mantle, pulling it over his nose and mouth.

For days Elijah trudged over the rugged terrain. He had nothing to eat, but neither was he hungry. When he reached the mountain he camped inside a cavern and continued to count the sunrises, the noontimes, and sunsets—forty days would pass before he would eat again.

It was a miracle, but even so Elijah's spirit was not lifted.

As ill-humored as ever, he thought about the Children of Israel camping at the foot of this same mountain, trembling with fear at the sound of God's voice thundering out the commandments. Struck with fear they begged Moses for relief. *How soon they forgot that voice and their God,* he thought bitterly. The cavern was like an echo chamber and he wished God would shout again so the cave would reverberate with firey words of judgment on Israel!

Wallowing in self-pity, out of the vast emptiness of the hollow cave he heard the Lord ask, "What are you doing here?"

And petulantly he answered, "I have been very zealous for the Lord God Almighty. The Israelites have rejected your covenant, broken down your altars, and put your prophets to death with the sword. I am the only one left, and now they are trying to kill me too."

God did not reply except to say, "Go out and stand on the mountain in the presence of the Lord, for the Lord is about to pass by."

Elijah did as he was told, and as he did he heard a ferocious roar and saw the black column of a whirlwind tearing rocks from the mountains, sending avalanches thundering down the valleys! The force of spinning winds battered him about, slammed him against the side of the cave.

As quickly as the storm came, it rushed past him. Elijah, shaken and afraid, glanced about. *Where is God? Why doesn't he speak?* The strange silence unnerved him.

Hardly had Elijah recovered from the wind when the ground beneath his feet began to move, throwing him off balance. Quickly the movement escalated, as if someone took hold of the earth and shook it violently! The deafening rumble of falling stones and crashing trees terrified him. After the first shock passed, tremors followed. Shocked and shaking, Elijah watched as surface cracks widened and boulders the size of a house slid down inside, swallowed whole!

As the dust settled Elijah's heart beat wildly. Cautiously he tried to get his bearings; and as he did he wondered where God was in all this. The Lord did not speak nor show himself in any way.

No sooner was the earthquake rumbling off in the distance than a forest fire roared up the mountainside—great billowing clouds of smoke rising high in the air. The heat of it burned his face and falling trees showered him with sparks. The crackling flames, racing where they pleased, mocked him as he trembled inside the cave.

Even after the fire had roared past him leaving the ground blackened and debris smoldering and smoking, his only thought was *where is God?* God was not in the fire either! Too weak to stand, Elijah slid down on the ground and sat with his head in his hands afraid for what would happen next.

Then, out of nowhere, Elijah heard a gentle whisper! He pulled his cloak around his face, and crawled cautiously toward the mouth of the cave. The voice said to him, "What are you doing here, Elijah?"

His answer was unchanged and, being well rehearsed during the long hours of solitude, he repeated it word for word. "I have been very zealous for the Lord God almighty. The Israelites have rejected your covenant, broken down your altars, and put your prophets to death with the sword. I am the only one left, and now they are trying to kill me too."

In retrospect, Elijah felt ashamed when he recalled his despair. God had not argued with him—merely told him to go to Damascus and anoint Hazael to be king over Syria. That order hit him in the pit of his stomach. Hazael was a wicked Israelite who would commit atrocities against Israel.

The Lord had other orders—the anointing of Jehu to be king of Israel, with instructions to destroy the house of Ahab and the prophets of Baal. And then God instructed Elijah to commission Elisha to take his place as head of the prophets. The die was cast. Elijah knew his ministry would soon end.

Then God answered Elijah's complaint, informing him, "Yet I reserve seven thousand in Israel—all whose knees have not bowed down to Baal and all whose mouths have not kissed him."

Elijah bowed in submission and carried out God's orders with a heavy heart.

Only in the matter of Naboth's vineyard, which Jezebel had obtained by having the owner and his sons killed, did Elijah prophesy to Ahab again. How vividly he remembered the encounter. Finding the king in the vineyard enjoying his new procurement, Elijah pronounced God's curse: Every male member of Ahab's family would die and not be buried. "Dogs will eat those belonging to Ahab who die in the city, and the birds of the air will feed on those who die in the country." As for Jezebel, she would die by the wall of Jezreel.

Ahab repented and, when he died in battle, God permitted him to be buried.

After that long night of remembering, Elijah's thoughts lingered with him. He shook Elisha awake and in half an hour they were on the road to Gilgal. As they walked the old prophet pondered how long it would be before the curse would fall on Ahab's sons. How soon would it be before Jezebel got her just dessert?

Only recently, Elijah had rebuked Ahab's son, Ahaziah, for consulting Philistine gods. In his rage Ahaziah had tried to arrest the prophet, and in answer Elijah had called down fire on the soldiers sent to take him.

It was a fitting climax to a lifetime of service. Yet Elijah had his regrets.

Another whirlwind was coming, he knew—not unlike the one at Sinai that had rent the rocks and sent them crashing down the mountainside. As he prepared to leave Gilgal, Elijah leaned on his staff. Looking at Elisha he said, "Stay here; the Lord has sent me to Bethel."

Elisha shook his head. "As surely as the Lord lives and as you live, I will not leave you."

So they went down to Bethel where a school for prophets was held. The young men lived there in a colony with their wives and called themselves "sons of the prophets." Elijah thought of them as his own family and if it was a matter of blood relation, one of them would be entitled to the birthright, a double portion of inheritance and with it, the leadership of the family. As it was, the relationship was spiritual and the birthright spiritual. The leadership would go to the man most deserving of it.

As they strode into Bethel, the students looked at them with awe. Excitedly, the young men took Elisha aside and asked him, "Do you know that the Lord is going to take your master from you today?"

"Yes, I know," Elisha answered, "but do not speak of it."

After conversing with the men there, Elijah rose to go. "Stay here, Elisha; the Lord has sent me to Jericho."

Elisha drew himself up his full height and with obvious determination replied, "As surely as the Lord lives and as you live, I will not leave you."

Elijah shook his head and started down the road. The city of palms was a beautiful prospect—perhaps he would be taken from there, he did not know. As they approached the fountains on the edge of the city the young men came out to meet them. Huddling around Elisha they asked, "Do you know that the Lord is going to take your master from you today?"

"Yes, I know," he replied, "but do not speak of it."

When his business in Jericho was finished, Elijah again told Elisha, "Stay here; the Lord has sent me to the Jordan."

Elisha stubbornly resisted. "As surely as the Lord lives and as you live, I will not leave you."

So the two of them walked on, and following at a short distance were fifty of the sons of the prophets. At the Jordan the two prophets hesitated, noting the sluggish stream glimmering in the afternoon sun. Elijah took off his cloak and, rolling it up, he drew it back and swatted the water. Immediately the river parted, making a path for them to cross.

Elijah did not look back but knew the men were marveling. They shouldn't. Had not God opened the Jordan for Joshua?

They were on a road heading east, and the imminence of his departure occupied their conversation. Elijah said to Elisha, "Tell me, what can I do for you before I am taken from you?"

Elisha was definite. "Let me inherit a double portion of your spirit."

"You have asked a difficult thing," Elijah said, "yet if you see me when I am taken from you, it will be yours—otherwise not."

Elisha made sure he kept in step with Elijah, and as they walked they talked, the way they always did when they were traveling. One of them was in the midst of a sentence when suddenly a chariot of fire and horses of fire passed between them and a whirlwind scooped up Elijah, snatching him out of sight! Elisha shouted, "My father! My father! The chariots and horsemen of Israel!"

Distraught at the loss of Israel's first line of defense, Elisha took hold of his own clothes and tore them apart.

Stunned and confused, Elisha did not at first see the cloak, but there it was—at his feet lay Elijah's mantle, the symbol of his authority as leader among the prophets. Trembling, Elisha picked up the garment and going back to the river, he looked across at the fifty young men watching him. Striking the water with the cloak, he cried out, "Where now is the Lord, the God of Elijah?"

Quietly, the water parted. Walking across the river on the narrow path, Elisha heard the men talking. One of them said, "The spirit of Elijah is resting on Elisha." As Elisha reached them, they made an appeal. "Look," they said, "we your servants have fifty able men. Let them go and look for your master. Perhaps the Spirit of the Lord has picked him up and set him down on some mountain or in some valley."

"No," Elisha replied, "do not send them."

But the young men insisted and finally Elisha let them go. For three days they searched the hills and valleys, walked along the streams, but they did not find Elijah. As they returned they found Elisha resting in Jericho and gave him their report. Elisha looked at them kindly. "Didn't I tell you not to go?"

Even today people have not given up looking for Elijah—not searching the hills beyond the Jordan, of course, but expecting him to return to earth. Did not the prophet Malachi promise his return?

Once three men saw Elijah standing on a mountain, conversing with Jesus Christ and Moses. They were talking about the death of Christ, which was soon to take place. Peter, James, and John recognized Elijah, although they'd never known him in life.

Did it make them wonder that this man Elijah, who prayed to die, has never died?

# Part IV

---

# New Testament Experiences

# 8

# The Widow's Son Comes Alive

GOD HAS COME TO HELP HIS PEOPLE.

Scripture Reference: Luke 7:11-18

The excitement he felt had not dimmed. Simon Peter could scarcely believe it yet, that Jesus had chosen him to be one of the Twelve. That Jesus had selected him to be among the Seventy he sent out before had been a great honor, but now this! There on the mountain Jesus had called for Simon Peter, Galilean fisherman; and when he climbed up to where Jesus was sitting he was told that he, along with eleven others, were chosen from among all the multitude of followers to be disciples.

The message Jesus gave the newly appointed men at that time was beyond Simon's comprehension—something about turning the other cheek—rejoicing when persecuted. When the little party came down on the plain Jesus repeated the message to the multitude. Simon Peter listened carefully, trying to remember the words so that he might ask his brother Andrew, or one of the others, if they understood.

The crowd followed Jesus to Capernaum, pushing and shoving, wanting to hear and see everything that was going on with the Nazarene. Their curiosity peaked when a Roman officer sent several Jews to ask Jesus to heal his servant. Simon Peter also wondered if Jesus would do anything for a Gentile. The Jewish messengers made a strong appeal for the centurion, arguing that he deserved the favor because he had befriended the Jews.

Peter was not surprised when Jesus healed the servant, but

he was somewhat baffled when Jesus commended the centurion. "I tell you," he said, "I have not found such great faith even in Israel."

A Sadducee in the crowd frowned, and Simon watched to see if he would say something. No Jew enjoyed being bested by a Gentile, least of all a religious Jew. Sadducees were especially religious; dogmatic about the scriptures, unalterably opposed to anything supernatural, notorious for rejecting the idea of resurrection. They vied with the Pharisees for dominance in religious matters and scorned the Pharisees' belief in immortality. For Jesus to rate a Roman officer above all Jews in matters of religion was an affront of the worst kind to a Sadducee.

Jesus moved through the gate of the city, leaving Capernaum, apparently to escape the crowd. But the crowd followed.

"Where're we going?" someone asked, and a girl replied, "This is the road to Nain."

Along the way they would see Mt. Tabor, a smooth mound against the sky, where the village of Nain rested two miles south. Simon Peter remembered Nain from his childhood, a pretty little town with a hillside just outside. As he remembered it, there were caves honeycombing the hillside and people buried their dead there.

The Apostle was striding ahead now, and when he glanced over his shoulder he saw James and John pushing their way through the crowd for the prestige of walking on either side of Jesus. He smiled to himself and followed close behind the Sadducee, who was arguing with the people around him.

After a while the crowd was rounding Mt. Tabor and people were tiring—some of them stopping to rest in the shade while others pressed on. A child, draped over his mother's shoulder, slept soundly, damp curls framing the soft round face. Perspiration trickled down Simon Peter's neck. He wiped his hand across his neck and thought how good a swim would feel. All around him the human smell was strong and he wished for a sea breeze.

In another hour they were nearing Nain, and children ran ahead to be the first to reach the town. *Good*, he thought. *The women will give us supper, and maybe we'll spend the night there.* He measured the sun in the sky and estimated there were three hours of daylight left.

Soon the children were running back, very excited and eager to tell what was up ahead.

So, a burial procession was on the way. Peter sighed. Everybody stopped for a funeral—custom said they must join it. All that weeping and wailing—Yes, he could hear them now; they sounded hysterical. Hired mourners, playing sad music on their instruments, caused women to beat their breasts, wail, and weep. Emotions ran rampant.

The commotion woke the baby on the mother's shoulder, making the poor child cry. Red in the face, he screamed, and nothing his mother did pacified him.

Peter could not see the bier but he was well aware of the woman following it—a widow. He could tell by her headdress. The crowd from Capernaum mingled with the bereaved and, by inquiring, learned details. "It's her only son who died," a woman said, visibly aggrieved.

As Jesus brushed past him, Peter glimpsed his face, soft and tender with compassion. *What's he going to do?* he wondered. *The man's dead.* Jesus was moving toward the litter. *Uh-oh, he'll have us all join the procession*, he thought.

The Apostle followed as closely as he could, and when he heard Jesus tell the woman not to weep, he wondered how he could say such a thing. With her son lying a corpse and all the lamentation going on, how could she not weep?

Jesus laid his hand on the stretcher and the men carrying it stopped. The body was swathed in linen and smelled fragrant from the myrrh. Without raising his voice Jesus spoke. "Young man, I say to you, get up!"

The crowd gasped—the corpse moved! Struggling to sit up, the man was trying to say something! The widow looked as if she would swoon; women came to her aid. Shock went through the crowd like a wave, and Peter felt a giddiness in his head. No man alive had ever seen such a thing!

Andrew pressed his brother forward to help unwrap the graveclothes. Working nervously, they both were all thumbs.

Once freed, the young man looked around as if in a daze. Then, stretching his limbs and yawning, he showed plainly he was alive! The mother, weeping for joy, embraced her son.

When people recovered their senses they began praising God. They kept saying, "A great prophet has appeared among us." And, "God has come to help his people."

Simon Peter eased between the bystanders; he wanted to see the Sadducee's face. There he was, not far from the bier. Peter caught his eye. The man scowled and turned his face away.

Simon Peter smiled to himself. The Sadducee would be hard put to deny what his eyes had seen.

In the excitement of welcoming the young man back to life—all the hugs and tears of well-wishers—Jesus had walked away. Andrew beckoned to his brother to come along.

# 9

# A Twelve-Year-Old Girl Lives Again

J udas Iscariot was troubled. He and the other disciples were following Jesus back to Capernaum and at that time, with John the Baptist in prison and Herod riled up, it seemed unwise—if not dangerous—to be going back into Herod's territory. After they secured the boat, they trudged along, wearied as much by the hangers-on as by the long road.

Judas reflected upon his lot. At the onset of his calling to discipleship Jesus had spoken at length about the Kingdom, and in the beginning Judas hoped the Rabbi would, indeed, take over the government. Now, as he remembered that sermon more carefully, he realized it was not a declaration of war but a declaration of revolution in behavior. *If that's all there is to the man's thinking,* Judas thought, *then Jesus is only a radical idealist.*

It wasn't that Jesus lacked courage—he lambasted the Pharisees for their hypocrisy, risking the wrath of the religious establishment, and he paid little respect to Jewish customs. He healed Gentiles as well as Jews and did not mind eating with Samaritans.

Judas had been amazed at the feats the Nazarene performed. He thought the raising of the man from the dead at Nain was most spectacular, but on this last trip he had seen two miracles that were equally spectacular. Sailing across the open sea, a violent windstorm threatened to capsize their boat and send them all to a watery grave. Jesus stood up, commanded the wind and waves to cease, and the storm stopped! Then no sooner did they arrive in the region of Gadara than a wild man came out of the tombs, shrieking and clawing at his flesh. Jesus cast a legion of demons out of the wretched man and sent them into swine feeding nearby. All those squealing pigs rushing down into the sea was a sight he'd never forget.

A woman interrupted Judas's train of thought. She was trying to squeeze between him and the fat man beside him to get closer to Jesus. White-faced, emaciated, she was obviously sick. Well, there was no way she could get near Jesus. Pressing in on all sides of the Rabbi were Pharisees and disciples of John. Judas caught the drift of the discussion—something about fasting. A kind of hush fell over the crowd and then he could hear clearly. Jesus was saying, "The time will come when the Bridegroom will be taken away from them; then they will fast.

"No one sews a patch of unshrunk cloth on an old garment, for the patch will pull away from the garment, making the tear worse. Neither do men pour new wine into old wineskins. If they do, the skins will burst, the wine will run out, and the wineskins will be ruined. No, they pour new wine into new wineskins, and both are preserved."

Judas frowned. Recently, Jesus had begun cloaking everything he said in parables, making it all a mystery, hard to understand.

Jesus stopped to talk to a man; the crowd pulled in close around him to see and hear. He was talking to the ruler of a synagogue in Capernaum. Judas knew the man well. He was named Jairus and he lived with his family next door to the synagogue. Seeing Jairus's distressed face, he knew he was desperate. "It's something about his daughter," the fat man muttered. "I guess she's sick or something."

*Well,* Judas thought, *if Jesus took my advice, he'd not dilly-dally this way. With the mood of the authorities being what it is, he should make himself shy in Galilee. Herod's arrested John the Baptist—next thing you know, it'll be us.*

The crowd began moving again, and in their rough, crude way they were jostling him. Judas felt the money pouch inside his girdle, cautious lest some pickpocket relieve him of its contents. There were only a few coins left—not enough for him to filch even one for himself without being discovered.

Judas knew he didn't belong in that inner circle of confidants, and it intrigued him that Jesus had chosen him. He enjoyed his privileged position because it gave him the opportunity, not only to make a few shekels for himself, but to observe firsthand this incredible Rabbi. Around the clock Judas watched his every move, heard every word he said, and it was amazing to him that Jesus never let down his guard—never wavered one iota. Judas smiled. *I wonder if he knows he has a spy among his ranks?*

Seeking a breath of air, Judas made his way to the fringe of the crowd. In his wake the sick woman was able to slip closer to Jesus. No sooner did Judas free himself from the press than Jesus called a halt. "Who touched my clothes?" he asked.

A twitter went through the crowd. *Whatever does he mean?* Judas wondered. One of the disciples spoke up, "You see the people crowding against you and yet you can ask, 'Who touched me?'"

Jesus kept looking about until the sick woman Judas had noticed before stepped forward. Judas craned his neck to see. "She's shaking like a leaf," someone said.

Judas couldn't see, but apparently the woman fell on the ground before Jesus. Everyone was trying to hear what she was saying. Judas couldn't hear everything she said, but the gist of it was that she'd been sick twelve years and had spent all her money on doctors but was no better. An issue of some kind—probably a woman's sickness—was the cause. She said she touched the fringe on Jesus' garment and was healed right away.

The crowd murmured excitedly. *Eager for more circus,*

Judas thought. *Well, I don't doubt he did it,* he said to himself. *The man can do wonders.*

Above the hubbub he heard Jesus say, "Daughter, your faith has healed you. Go in peace and be freed from your suffering."

During the excitement someone from Jairus's house arrived and drew the ruler aside. The messenger dropped his eyes to the ground, reluctant to tell him. Jairus grabbed him by the shoulders, forcing him to speak.

"Your daughter is dead," he told him, his face drawn with the pain of saying it. Jairus, distraught, whirled around toward Jesus. The messenger clutched his arm. "Why bother the teacher any more?"

But Jesus was making his way toward Jairus. "Don't be afraid; just believe," he told him.

The messenger shook his head. "He doesn't understand."

Moving faster, the crowd reached the city gate and surged past the vendors there. Through a maze of streets they followed Jairus excited by the prospect of what might happen.

Even before they reached Jairus's house the sounds of weeping and wailing reached their ears. Thin pipes were sounding mournful lamentations, wrenching heartsobs from those gathered to grieve the passing of the girl. The mourning would continue seven days with hysteria mounting every day.

When they reached the house Jairus took Jesus and the disciples inside. Three rows of women on either side of the room faced each other, clapping their hands and striking their breasts in time to a monotone chant. One side, led by an old woman, sang the praises of the dead girl, while the other answered in response. Then they shrieked and wailed, making a rattling noise in their throats while the distraught mother kneeled on the floor, swaying back and forth, joining in the wild cry.

A mourner flung herself prostrate on the floor, hair disheveled, clothes ripped and in disarray, her face daubed with dirt and paint. In a paroxysm of grief other women danced around her, contorting their limbs, their bodies swaying in a melancholy trance to the jangle of tambourines. An old hag called out the virtues of the girl, calling her by names of endearment and plaintively mourning her departure.

A minstrel began beating one of the tambourines in a solemn measure, and the company began clapping their hands in rhythmn, saying, "Alas, for her! Alas, for her! She was sweet, she was good; alas for her!"

Seeing the visitors, the mourners tried to engage them in the emotional display.

Jesus intruded upon their orchestrated fanfare to the obvious displeasure of the women. "Why all this commotion and wailing?" he asked. "The child is not dead but asleep."

They laughed and hooted at that.

Jesus motioned them outside. Unwillingly they relented and filed past him churlishly. Angry as they were, they would not stay on the premises. With the room vacated except for the disciples and the girl's family, Jesus took Jairus and his wife and Peter, James, and John, and they went into the room where the body lay.

The rest of the Twelve milled about the courtyard waiting for the outcome, but the crowd, sympathetic with the mourners, left. Judas pretended to draw himself a drink of water from a jar and add a little wine as the custom was. In fact, he took his wine without water. Pouring the wine from the skin he thought again of Jesus' words: "New wine in old wineskins . . ." *Hmmmn, new wine is not as good as this,* he thought as he swirled the drink in his mouth.

Judas then sipped the cup leisurely, and by the time he was done, he could hear them coming out of the girl's room.

He followed the other disciples back inside. It took a minute for his eyes to become accustomed to the dimness; but when he could see, there was the girl standing beside her mother! She was waiting for the food the woman was preparing.

The men were amazed, and as Jesus was telling them not

to tell anyone what had happened, they were hardly paying attention.

Seeing that the family wished to be alone, the disciples went outside again. Judas was anxious to ask what happened but bided his time. Shortly, he overheard James and John explaining, "He took her by the hand, and said, 'My child, get up,' and she did!"

"I'd say she's about twelve years old, wouldn't you, John?"

"Yes. She's twelve," his brother affirmed.

"Was she really dead?" Judas asked.

"Absolutely!"

"How can we keep something like this quiet?" James wanted to know. "People will see her playing in the yard."

"There's no way," they all agreed.

"But maybe we can get away from here before the news breaks."

Jesus came out of the house and, walking across the yard, headed for the road. Judas fell in behind him with the rest of them.

# 10

# A Decayed Body Is Raised

TAKE OFF THE GRAVE CLOTHES AND LET HIM GO.

Scripture Reference Luke 16:19-31; 17:11-37; John 11:1-46

From Thomas's way of thinking, they got out of Judea none too soon. At the Feast of Dedication Jesus had caused an uproar and might have been stoned had he not escaped in the nick of time. Crossing the Jordan he and the disciples came into Perea. There they traversed the area, listened to Jesus teach, watched him perform miracles.

When someone warned Jesus that Herod was threatening to apprehend him he shrugged it off, calling the governor a fox. But, as much as their imminent danger bothered Thomas, he was bothered more by what the Lord was telling them.

Among other things Jesus laid down the requirements for discipleship—counting the cost, that sort of thing. And there was the matter of all these parables: on the surface prosaic little stories, but in reality so profound as to be mind boggling. Sometimes Thomas could not tell if what Jesus was saying was a parable or something that actually happened.

Thomas was glad they were stopping for the day. Beneath the shadow of the great rock behind him there was a welcome coolness. The desert area of Perea would be a no-man's-land except for the traffic to and from Judea and Galilee. No self-respecting Jew crossed Samaritan territory, and to avoid Samaria one had to cross the Jordan and take the road on the eastern side through Perea.

Unlike more religious Jews Thomas was not as prejudiced against Samaritans. He had known some who were decent, good fellows. Of course, they were half-breeds. The Jewish blood in them was from the inferiors left behind in the land when Israel was exiled, and their heathen parentage came from the poor victims of war, conquered people brought in from other countries to settle the Promised Land.

Their ancestry explained their religious heresies. When the Exile ended, because the Samaritans were of mixed blood the Jews would not allow them to help rebuild Jerusalem. This caused the Samaritans to build themselves a temple on Mt. Gerizim. The rival place of worship and their lack of respect for Jewish legalisms made the Samaritans untouchables.


Thomas, a heavy man, stretched out on the ground, closed his eyes, and waited for the sun to go down. As his mind idled one after another of the stories Jesus told floated in his head. The one most vivid lingered for some time. It was about a rich man and a beggar—how the beggar was laid at the rich man's gate, full of sores, dogs licking them. Thomas remembered just such a beggar in Capernaum, emaciated, repulsive, asking alms by the synagogue. Not a pleasant picture.

In time both men died—the beggar, Lazarus, going to heaven accompanied by angels; the rich man to torment.

Just like that! One minute breathing in, the next breathing out, and in an instant either with the blessed dead or in torment. No reason given. One to Abraham's bosom, the other to flames of fire.

Thomas covered his eyes with his arm and tried to figure it out.

He considered that place Jesus was talking about was Hades. A Greek merchant, a God-fearer, had explained Hades to Thomas—the place of departed spirits, he had said. Well, maybe so. Thomas understood Greek and spoke Aramaic, yet he could not hold his own with smart men like the merchant. If there was such a place as Hades, with part of it Paradise and the other part Torment, Jesus' story described precisely that.

And, he was fascinated by the idea that those in Paradise were *visible* to those in Torment.

In his mind Thomas went over the story one piece at a time. The rich man cries out to Abraham for mercy: "Father Abraham, have pity on me and send Lazarus to dip the tip of his finger in water and cool my tongue, because I am in agony in this fire."

Thomas found it hard to believe—Abraham refused the rich man's request. "Son," Abraham said, "remember that in your lifetime you received your good things, while Lazarus received bad things, but now he is comforted here and you are in agony."

The explanation disturbed Thomas. It implied some kind of virtue in being poor, in suffering, and condemnation for being prosperous. *That can't be right,* he thought. *Abraham himself was rich; Job, David, many other great believers were rich . . . Perhaps the rich man was selfish or crooked or both and Lazarus was righteous.*

An ant was crawling on his arm. Unconsciously he brushed it off. *It's obvious,* he reasoned, *that the rich man should have done more for Lazarus than give him the scraps from his table. Tells you something about a man if he can't take the time to help someone less fortunate, someone who's suffering.*

The more he thought about the loose ends in the story, the more convinced he became that Jesus didn't tell the story to show the way to Paradise but to describe the state beyond the grave.

Thomas tried to visualize Hades in his mind—Paradise on one side, Torment on the other, with an insurmountable space between. Abraham called it a "great chasm," one that prevented traffic either way: "So that those who want to go from here to you cannot, nor can anyone cross over from there to us."

In his reverie Thomas thought of Samaria as the "great chasm" not to be crossed; and realizing how tired he was he tried to think more clearly.

The sun had dropped behind the mountains on the western side of the river, and the lengthened shadows were fusing into dusk. Soon Jesus and all the disciples would be lying down to sleep. Thomas envied how easily the others could sleep. As for himself, once he had a perplexing matter on his mind, he could not rest until he came to some kind of satisfactory conclusion. That was what made him restless, insecure, sometimes moody, frustrated, because he could not always find the answers.

That rich man in Torment troubled him. How could a disembodied spirit burn? Was Jesus talking figuratively or did he mean the soul assumes a body of sorts that can burn? Are the wicked resurrected, their bodies also made immortal in order to burn? It was too much for him to fathom and Thomas wasn't prepared to ask the Rabbi.

*Imagine,* he thought, *suffering the flames, asking for a drop of water and being refused! No second chance—not even a drop of water! No wonder the rich man begged Abraham to send Lazarus to warn his brothers so they wouldn't share his fate. But even that was denied!* He recalled that Abraham said, "They have Moses and the Prophets; let them listen to them."

*He means the Torah,* Thomas told himself. *It's silly to expect busy men of the world to read the Law. It's true that every Jew knows he's held accountable for the teachings of Moses and the Prophets, but the only Jews I know who read for themselves are rabbis, priests, or scribes.*

The rich man had argued just that point. "No, father Abraham," the rich man said, "but if someone from the dead goes to them, they will repent."

Thomas could not agree with that. A resurrected Lazarus would not convince the brothers. He knew from experience for he had seen two people raised from the dead, but he hadn't learned anything from them. Neither the man at Nain nor the daughter of Jairus had warned of a Torment to come nor talked about a Paradise. Even if they had he would not put faith in what they said. After all, he reasoned, when somebody's so sick they die (!), who's to say they aren't mentally wandering or suffering effects of laudanum?

Besides, the two Jesus raised were dead such a short time—the girl was still lying on her bed; the fellow, raised the same day he died. It might make a difference if someone who'd been dead a long time were actually to come out of the grave. The resurrection of someone whose flesh was decaying—that would be impressive, to say the least.

One by one the disciples spread their pallets and lay down to sleep. Thomas studied on the matter, shifting from one side to the other, trying to get comfortable. Under the shelter of the rock he did not feel the wind, but the chill made him pull up his cloak about his shoulders. Surrounded by mounds of individual bodies, he listened as one after another of his friends succumbed to sleep, their breathing labored from fatigue. Covering his ears to shut out the snoring, he still could not sleep.

Thomas gazed out over the desert. In the clear night air the brilliance of the stars shone with dazzling clarity, making him wonder what lay beyond them . . .

Sometime before dawn he finally drifted off to sleep.

During the days that followed the disciples and Jesus roamed about—first on the border of Galilee and Samaria, then back into Perea again. Jesus healed ten lepers, and of the ten only one returned to thank him. Ironically the man was a Samaritan, and Thomas was curious to know if James or John felt chagrined by that. Those sons of Zebedee were openly hostile toward Samaritans. It seemed to Thomas that Jesus went out of his way to put Samaritans in a good light. He remembered Jesus talking with the woman at Jacob's well, and the night they spent in her Samaritan village. And only recently Jesus had told a parable about a Samaritan who showed kindness to a victim on the Jericho road. It troubled Thomas that Jesus was so liberal in his views; it could only lead to confrontation with the Jewish leaders.

They were fording a stream and the others were far ahead of him. In the heat and with his weight, he couldn't keep up with them. *And, perhaps,* he said to himself, *all this contemplation slows me down.*

Coming up on the other side of the stream he said, "Now where was I? Oh, yes, confrontation with the Jewish leaders." *Of course,* he thought, *Jesus always gets the better of them in debate. His answers to their questions are profound, and I'm as much impressed by the things Jesus says and the way he says them as by what he does.* Thomas recalled how the Pharisees wanted to know when the Kingdom of God would come, and Jesus dumbfounded them by saying the Kingdom was in their midst.

Thomas couldn't understand that. *Surely the Pharisees are not members of God's Kingdom—Jesus made that clear when he called them hypocrites. What did he mean? Did he mean he is the king and where the king is, there is the kingdom?*

The answer sounded reasonable, and Thomas let the question rest.

But then there was the most disturbing matter of all: Jesus said he was going to leave them. That Thomas could understand; but then Jesus said he would come back. His return would be sudden, as in the days of Noah when the flood came, and as in the time of Lot when fire and brimstone fell. Jesus said two people would be sleeping in one bed, one would be taken and the other left.

When somebody asked, "Where?" all Jesus said was, "Where there is a dead body, there the vultures will gather."

Well, of course, vultures gather in the sky—*is that what he means?* Thomas wondered. *Will people be taken up in the sky, caught up like Enoch, like Elijah?*

The questions raised gave him a weariness of mind. Thomas longed for their less complicated beginning, the less threatening days when the disciples first began following Jesus—when enthusiasms ran high, and pressures were not so great. What good times they had enjoyed in Bethany, eating at Martha's table, going with the sisters and brother to the village well; resting in the shade of the olive tree by the pool in the courtyard. The other sister, Mary, was so devoted to Jesus she hung onto his every word. A sweet and godly woman, Mary.

They were rounding a bend in the road, Thomas straggling along last in line, when he heard someone yelling to them from behind. He looked back down the road, and someone was running to catch up with them, waving his arms. Thomas thought that coming from the south, he might well be bringing news from Judea.

The men stopped in the road and waited for him. As he drew closer, Thomas recognized him as a fellow they knew in Bethany. Apparently he'd been running hard for some time; by the time he reached them he was near collapse. Gasping for breath, he could hardly get out the words. "Lord, the one you love is sick."

That could mean only Lazarus, brother of Martha and Mary. Thomas didn't like the sound of it. They all loved Lazarus like a brother, but Bethany was too close to Jerusalem to be safe for them. Surely Jesus won't risk going to Bethany!

He didn't. All Jesus said to the messenger was, "This sickness will not end in death. No, it is for God's glory so that God's Son may be glorified through it."

Thomas heaved a sigh of relief!

Early the next morning, after the messenger had rested, he left, taking Jesus' message back to the sisters in Bethany.

For the next two days Jesus continued business as usual. Knowing how devoted he was to Lazarus it was difficult to understand his calm indifference; but Thomas was so relieved that they were staying in Perea, he did not raise a question.

In fact all the disciples had relaxed, assuming that Jesus had no intention of risking the trip south, when abruptly he announced, "Let us go back to Judea."

Immediately they protested. "But Rabbi, a short while ago

the Jews tried to stone you, and yet you are going back there?"

Jesus told them he knew what he was doing—that he was walking in light they apparently did not have. Besides, he told them, "Our friend Lazarus has fallen asleep; but I am going there to wake him up."

The disciples looked at one another, appalled. "Lord, if he sleeps, he will get better."

"Lazarus is dead," Jesus said, "and for your sake I am glad I was not there, so that you may believe. But let us go to him."

Thomas gathered his things together and moved along with the rest of the disciples. Shaking his head he muttered under his breath to the others, "Let us also go, that we may die with him."

They traveled all day and when they arrived near Bethany they found that Lazarus had already been in the tomb four days. Thomas felt conscience-stricken. It was really too bad. Lazarus was a true friend. If Jesus knew he was going to Bethany anyway, why didn't he go before Lazarus died? He could have healed him as easily as he healed the lepers.

Knowing there would be a swarm of mourners at the house, Jesus had them stop short of the town and wait for the sisters to come out to them. It wasn't long before Martha came, but Mary stayed at home.

The first thing Martha said was exactly what Thomas had been thinking. "Lord, if you had been here, my brother would not have died." Her eyes were red from crying and there was a catch in her voice as she added, "But I know that even now God will give you whatever you ask."

"Your brother will rise again," he said.

"I know he will rise again in the resurrection at the last day."

Thomas sensed the tension in Martha's voice.

"I am the resurrection and the life," Jesus told her. "He who believes in me will live, even though he dies; and whoever lives and believes in me will never die. Do you believe this?"

The Rabbi waited for her response and the disciples looked on, not knowing what to expect.

"Yes, Lord," she told him, "I believe that you are the Christ, the Son of God, who was to come into the world."

*It is the answer Simon Peter might have given*, Thomas thought.

Quickly glancing about Martha nodded to each of them, then left them waiting there while she went to fetch Mary.

When the two women returned there were others with them, curious mourners wanting to see the women grieve. Among them Thomas spotted several avowed enemies who had been at the Feast of Dedication; it made him cold with fear.

Mary had fallen at Jesus' feet. Finally she spoke. "Lord, if you had been here, my brother would not have died." She used the identical words Martha had used—*a dead giveaway*, Thomas thought. Obviously the two women had commiserated, and in their distress expressed the same thought to each other repeatedly.

If Mary was rebuking him, Jesus gave no defense. It was plain to see he was troubled—Thomas could see it in his face—as if he groaned inwardly. "Where have you laid him?" Jesus asked.

"Come and see, Lord," both the sisters said at once.

Then Thomas saw tears washing down Jesus' cheeks—a flood of them—a lump rose in his own throat. It was hard enough seeing the women weeping, the Jews lamenting; and he, too, felt miserable, for Lazarus was also his friend; but seeing Jesus weep was almost unbearable. Thomas had never seen him so anguished.

The crowd was excited by Jesus' tears. "See how he loved him," someone said, and it was repeated all around like some maudlin echo.

Their sentiment was dispelled by the voice of a man growling, "Could not he who opened the eyes of the blind man have kept this man from dying?"

He was undoubtedly one of the enemies from Jerusalem and a knot of fear tightened in Thomas's chest. Jesus, so deeply moved he seemed not to hear the man, moved slowly toward the tomb. In silence they stared at the limestone cave sealed with a stone. The finality of the grave brought more tears from the women, and Thomas swallowed hard to control his own feelings.

"Take away the stone," Jesus said.

Thomas couldn't believe his ears!

"But, Lord," said Martha, "by this time there will be a bad odor, for he has been buried four days."

It would be bad, Thomas agreed. Rotting flesh was the foulest odor he had ever smelled, and he didn't see any earthly reason why Jesus wanted the stone rolled away.

As he waited to see what would happen Martha's words, "four days," resounded in his head. His mind began calculating the time that had elapsed since first they heard that Lazarus was sick. After the messenger came to them, Jesus waited two days before doing anything. Then it took them a day to walk to Bethany. And, if it took them a day to walk to Bethany, it took the messenger a day to walk to Perea. He counted backward in his mind—one day for the messenger to reach them; two days waiting; one day to reach Bethany—four days. That means Lazarus had been dead when the messenger arrived!

With a swiftness that surprised him Thomas understood clearly—when the messenger reached them in Perea, Jesus knew Lazarus was already dead! Thomas checked his figures again to make sure. Satisfied that he was right, he felt confused. Trying to remember what Jesus had said when they were still in Perea, Thomas wondered what his words, "I am going there to wake him up," might mean. Could it be—?

The Rabbi was speaking to Martha. "Did I not tell you that if you believed, you would see the glory of God?"

Several men rushed forward and, putting their strength to the stone, pushed until it budged a bit. Taking a fresh start they steadily moved the stone aside and as the opening widened, the stench emitted was stifling! Thomas held his nose and stared at the black hole, straining to see inside.

Jesus stepped forward, all eyes upon him. He turned to look upward and as he did, he began talking to God. "Father, I thank you that you have heard me. I knew that you always hear me, but I said this for the benefit of the people standing here, that they may believe that you sent me."

Thomas's heart was thumping in his chest with such force he could hear it!

Jesus shouted, "Lazarus, come out!"

Thomas jumped back, but the mob leaning forward to see, held him right where he was.

Immediately there was a stirring inside the cave—Lazarus swinging his limbs down from the shelf onto the floor. Seeing that, people fell back from the cave, terrified. A girl swooned. Lazarus was struggling, his body swathed in linen strips, his face bound round with a cloth.

Only Jesus was calm. "Take off the grave clothes and let him go," he commanded.

Thomas felt his limbs trembling as he moved forward to help Lazarus. Other hands helped him unwrap the grave clothes. Nervously they unbound him, yard upon yard, leaving only his loins covered.

Lazarus, dazed, groped in the semi-darkness trying to get his bearings. The men led him outside and, seeing he was steady, they stepped aside. In the dazzling sunshine Lazarus covered his eyes with his arm until he grew accustomed to the light.

Mary and Martha clung to each other trembling, color drained from their faces, not believing their eyes. As they watched, the animated form of their brother took one step, then another.

The people, too, stood staring, taking no notice of someone pushing through the crowd to get away. Thomas glimpsed the man's face—a man he knew to be an informer! He watched as the informer broke free, then raced down the road. *No doubt about his mission.* Thomas thought, *Within half an hour he'll take this news to the Pharisees!*

Excited whispers started in the crowd. Heads nodded approvingly; admiring gazes followed Jesus. Then the sisters moved to embrace their brother. No longer able to contain their exuberance, friends crowded around the three, exclaiming praise to God and weeping tears of joy.

Thomas saw Jesus slipping away unnoticed by the crowd, and he disengaged himself to follow him.

# Part V

---

# The Death, Resurrection, and Ascenscion of Jesus

# 11

# The Predictions

HE BEGAN TO TEACH THEM . . . THAT HE MUST BE
KILLED AND AFTER THREE DAYS RISE AGAIN.

Scripture Reference: Matthew 16:13–17:23;
20:17–28; Mark 10:32–45; Matthew 27:63

The Tetrachy of Philip was rough country, the people more Gentile than Jewish, but frankly Matthew welcomed the relief from the pressures experienced in Galilee. The Galileans were getting so out of hand Jesus was forced to heal their sick in secret. In Bethsaida Jesus took a blind man outside the village, spit on his eyes, laid his hands on him, and asked if he could see. The man was only partially healed—saw people like trees walking around. Once more Jesus put his hands on the man's eyes, then he could see clearly. Jesus forbade him to return to the village, knowing the news of his healing would bring on a stampede of sick and afflicted sufferers. That's when Jesus and the disciples left, heading for the villages of Caesarea Philippi.

They were hurrying. If past experience taught anything it told them the healed man would make a bee-line for home; and if they didn't hurry they'd be overtaken by people swarming like locusts.

Putting a safe distance between themselves and Bethsaida, they relaxed and walked at a steady but easy pace. Jesus was asking them something and Matthew, on the fringe of the group, cupped his ear to hear. "Who do people say I am?"

Hesitating to formulate an answer, the Twelve exchanged

glances and several voiced what they had heard. "Some say John the Baptist; others say Elijah; and still others, one of the prophets."

"But what about you?" he asked. "Who do you say I am?"

Matthew didn't feel that he should give answer. There were others who were more outspoken than he.

Simon Peter ran his fingers through his hair, glanced around to see if anyone else was going to say anything, then in that booming voice of his he said, "You are the Christ," and his confidence was astounding.

Matthew was satisfied with that answer, but what followed was very disturbing to him. Jesus began telling them that the Son of Man would suffer many things and be rejected by the elders, chief priests, and teachers of the law. That much Matthew could accept, but then Jesus said that he must be killed and after three days rise again. The idea was so repugnant to Matthew he didn't want to think he heard correctly; but seeing the consternation on the faces of the other disciples, he realized that indeed Jesus had said he was going to die.

Simon Peter was at Jesus' elbow, nudging him aside. They walked a stone's throw away but their voices carried. Peter was remonstrating with Jesus. "Never, Lord! This shall never happen to you!"

Jesus turned, looked sternly at Simon, "Out of my sight, Satan! You are a stumbling block to me; you do not have in mind the things of God, but the things of men."

The sharp rebuke shocked Matthew. *Whatever does he mean*, he wondered, *calling Simon, Satan? Peter meant well.*

Jesus came back to the disciples, leaving Simon stunned and bewildered. "If anyone would come after me," the Lord said, "he must deny himself and take up his cross and follow me. For whoever wants to save his life will lose it, but whoever loses his life for me will find it."

The words were ominous and made Matthew uncomfortable. *A man does not carry a cross unless he expects to die on it. What does Jesus mean?*

Andrew looked at Matthew, raised his eyebrows questioningly. Speaking in a near whisper, he asked, "What does he mean—if you save your life you'll lose it?"

Matthew shrugged his shoulders. "He's talking in riddles."

"What good will it be for a man if he gains the whole world, yet forfeits his soul?" Jesus asked. "Or what can a man give in exchange for his soul?"

Again Andrew raised his eyebrows, and Matthew tried to explain. "Well, I think I understand what that means. A man should value his soul above material gain. That's exactly why I left the customs house. When Jesus said, 'Follow me,' I was ready to give it all up for the sake of my soul."

Andrew agreed. "That's the way I understand it."

They were coming to a fig tree that offered shade enough for them all, and Matthew was glad they were stopping to rest. He joined the others sitting down. Jesus was telling them something he'd mentioned before, something that intrigued Matthew for its mystery.

"For the Son of Man is going to come in his Father's glory with his angels, and then he will reward each person according to what he has done. I tell you the truth, some who are standing here will not taste death before they see the Son of Man coming in his kingdom."

The subject always disturbed Matthew. *I wish I understood what he means,* he thought. *I'd like to ask him, but after the way he rebuked Peter, I'm afraid . . . There's no telling how he might react . . . Then again, maybe not.*

Six days passed and still Matthew puzzled over the words, "some standing here will not taste death until they see the Son of Man coming in his kingdom." *I wonder if I'll be one of those who'll see him coming in the glory of his kingdom?*

The Lord and his disciples had returned to Galilee and were making camp at the foot of a very high mountain when

Jesus announced that he was going up on the mountain to pray. Matthew knew he wasn't up to climbing any mountain, tired as he was. A good night's sleep was what he needed. Besides, a crowd would come sooner or later and they would need all the attention the disciples could give. Lying by the fire, through half-closed eyes he watched to see if anyone would go with Jesus. First John got up, brushed himself off, and fell in behind Jesus. Of course James, his brother, would not be out-done; and as he headed up the mountain Simon Peter joined them.

Matthew smiled and closed his eyes. Those three were very much alike, never satisfied unless they were up front with Jesus. Matthew felt he was a more practical man, less given to solitude, to meditation and prayer. As a tax collector it had always been his policy to take care of business first, and if there was time for the other, all well and good. He had never been able to make religious duties a priority because feast times were his busiest seasons. Now, following Jesus about the country, his manner of life was definitely changing. He'd enjoyed Pass-over for the first time in years.

The next morning, just as Matthew predicted, a crowd of people had gathered looking for Jesus. Matthew was rolling up his sleeping mat when he heard an argument of some kind going on. He deliberately unrolled the sleeping mat and lay down again. He wanted no part of a fight.

Thomas and Thaddeus were talking with some scribes—the quarrel getting louder and the argument heating up. Mat-thew covered his ears and hoped to stay out of it. Then he heard scuffling—some jeering—a lot of commotion. Not want-ing to get involved he lazily let himself see what he could through narrow slits of his eyelids. In the midst of a knot of people somebody on the ground was stirring up dust. "He's having another fit!" a girl shouted, and more people came running to see the spectacle.

*Not that,* Matthew groaned to himself. *I guess I better see if I can help.*

Elbowing his way through the crowd, he watched as a youth, caught in the paroxysm of seizure, jerked about on the ground. Drooling at the mouth the victim stiffened, contorting his body and making unearthly sounds.

A spectator was eager to tell Matthew what the argument was about. Thomas, Thaddeus, and several of the others had laid hands on the youth in an effort to heal him, but nothing happened.

The scribes were having a field day.

"You try, Matthew," Thaddeus said.

Matthew wet his lips. If they couldn't heal the boy, he was sure he couldn't. He kneeled down beside the pitiful youth, who was slobbering at the mouth, his eyes glassy. Matthew laid his hands on the boy's head and pronounced the name of Jesus over him.

Suddenly the boy jerked convulsively and there was no stopping the terrible spasms that wrenched his body. Matthew stood up and backed away.

All morning the contest continued, first one disciple then another attempted to heal the boy. Perspiration poured off Philip as he tried again and again to cast out the demon tormenting the youth. With each try the ridicule of the onlookers became more vicious. Red in the face from the heat, angry and embarrassed, Philip finally gave up and flung himself down under a tree.

Matthew did not take another turn. He knew his limitations and would not make a fool of himself, yet he thought it strange that none of them was successful. They had cast out demons before; he remembered the great excitement they felt when they first discovered that demons were subject to them in Jesus' name.

The crowd grew tired of watching and went off down the road to a spring where there was water and some shade. The scribes continued hurling accusations at the defeated, frustrated disciples and tempers flared. "I don't understand it," Andrew complained, "we've done it before—we've cast out demons. I wish Jesus was here."

"They should be back today. They've been up there all night."

Matthew went over to comfort the father. The boy lay limp beside him, his countenance dazed, cuts and bruises all over his body. The poor man was exhausted. "I don't know how I'll get him home," he said. "He's worse today than usual." Despair made him sigh repeatedly. "We've tried everything. Nothing helps." His drooping shoulders sagged the more and his tearless eyes voiced the hopelessness of his soul.

Matthew wished for Jesus and kept looking up the trail for some sign of his return. The slant of shadows lengthened as the birds of prey began their evening vigil from the tops of trees. A hawk, perched high above him, reminded Matthew of the sinister surveillance of the scribes, always ready to pounce on the slightest weakness, the smallest failure. They would not let up; and seeing they had the upper hand they followed the disciples about, arguing vehemently for the benefit of the crowd.

Still no sign of Jesus. Matthew went to the spring and brought back a drink of water for the father and the boy. He offered the man bread but he refused, too heartsick to eat. Just as Matthew was putting the loaf back in his knapsack someone said, "Here comes Jesus."

James and John led the way down the mountain and striding past Matthew they did not so much as notice him. Such preoccupation was not like them. Jesus came next; then Matthew saw Simon, his eyes so intense it startled him—something extraordinary must have happened on that mountain. "What happened?" he asked.

Simon Peter shook his head, then paused long enough to say, "He charged us to tell no man what we've seen until the Son of Man has risen again from the dead."

"What do you mean, 'risen again from the dead'?" Peter brushed him aside. "I say," Matthew persisted, "what did you see up there? What happened?" He ran alongside Peter as he followed Jesus.

Reaching the disciples disputing with the scribes, Jesus asked, "What are you arguing with them about?"

The father of the boy was struggling to get up from where he was sitting.

"Teacher," he said, his plaintive voice strained, "I brought you my son, who is possessed by a spirit that has robbed him of speech. Whenever it seizes him it throws him to the ground. He foams at the mouth, gnashes his teeth, and becomes rigid. I asked your disciples to drive out the spirit, but they could not."

"Oh, unbelieving generation," Jesus replied, "how long shall I stay with you? How long shall I put up with you? Bring the boy to me."

Men were quick to lift the youth to his feet, and supported him as he tried to walk. Suddenly he was thrown down on the ground in another convulsion, and Matthew turned his face away, sick of watching the boy rolling on the ground, foaming at the mouth.

Jesus asked the father, "How long has he been like this?"

"From childhood," he answered. "It has often thrown him into fire or water to kill him. But if you can do anything take pity on us and help us."

" 'If you can'?" Jesus repeated, questioningly. "Everything is possible for him who believes."

"I do believe," the poor man cried, "help me overcome my unbelief!"

A flock of people were running up from the spring. Seeing them coming, Jesus quickly commanded the spirit to leave. "You deaf and dumb spirit," he said, "I command you, come out of him and never enter him again."

The spirit shrieked, convulsing the youth as it came out. The boy was knocked about, then thrown on the ground. There he lay as still as a stone. His face colorless, his breathing barely noticeable, people in the crowd began saying, "He's dead!"

But Jesus took the boy by the hand and stood him on his feet.

While the crowd marveled and the father wept for joy, Jesus slipped away. With the disciples following they made a swift retreat to a house far off the road.

When the door was closed behind them and they were once again alone, the disciples sat around looking sheepish. Matthew felt the shame intensely and could not look Jesus in the eye. Finally someone mustered the courage to ask, "Why couldn't we drive it out?"

"This kind can come out only by prayer."

Matthew hung his head.

After a few hours rest Jesus got up from the mat he was sleeping on, and one by one the others woke up. Jesus was intent on having time alone with the disciples to teach them, and in order to do that they had to escape the crowd. They slipped out of the house while the stars were still in the heavens and by daybreak they had put miles between themselves and the multitude.

Matthew was walking beside Judas, and Peter was alongside. Jesus broke the silence. "The Son of Man is going to be betrayed into the hands of men. They will kill him, and after three days he will rise."

Matthew looked at Judas, but his face registered nothing. He glanced at Peter, who was slowly shaking his head.

" 'Kill him?' " Matthew repeated. The matter so troubled him, he tried to put it out of his mind. But that was not possible; there were too many indications that Jesus' life was in danger. When they had left Galilee to go to Judea and were refused hospitality in a Samaritan village, James and John were furious. Now as he thought of it the refusal seemed ominous; for at the Feast of Tabernacles and, later, at the Feast of Dedication, the hostility intensified.

When Jesus had finally decided to leave Judea and travel to Perea, Matthew was relieved. There the tension was eased. Jesus taught the disciples parables, dined with a Pharisee, healed a few lepers. In fact, the only disturbing interruption was the return to Bethany where Jesus raised Lazarus from the dead. The furor that followed that sensational event drove them back to Perea.

Now again life was pleasant and they did not feel threatened. Jesus took time with little children, talked with a young man who was rich and prominent. Everything seemed to be running smoothly when Jesus announced abruptly, "We are going to Jerusalem, and everything that is written by the prophets about the Son of Man will be fulfilled. He will be handed over to the Gentiles. They will mock him, insult him, spit on him, flog him, and kill him. On the third day he will rise again."

Matthew looked from one man to another. It was obvious that they, too, did not know what Jesus was talking about. It was as if a dense fog settled on their understanding and they could not penetrate it. What concerned Matthew more than anything else was that they were going back to Jerusalem, a hotbed of opposition.

As they walked along James and John had their heads together. Their mother, Salome, joined them talking intensely, nodding her head. In a few minutes they had caught up with Jesus. "Teacher," they said, "we want you to do for us whatever we ask."

"What do you want me to do for you?" he asked.

"Let one of us sit at your right and the other at your left in your glory."

"You don't know what you are asking," Jesus said. "Can you drink the cup I drink or be baptized with the baptism I am baptized with?"

"We can," they answered, smiling with self-assurance.

"You will drink the cup I drink and be baptized with the baptism I am baptized with, but to sit on my right or left is not for me to grant. These places belong to those for whom they have been prepared."

The brothers' request did not set well with any of the Twelve. The face of Judas flushed, but he was not a man to say much. The others didn't mind saying what they thought, and Matthew could see a loud and heated discussion coming. Well, he would not get into it. *If anyone is qualified for rank in the kingdom, it is I,* he thought. *What do fishermen know about running a government?*

Quietly Jesus addressed himself to the subject. "You know that those who are regarded as rulers of the Gentiles lord it over them, and their high officials exercise authority over them. Not so with you."

*Well, all right,* Matthew told himself, *if that's the way he wants it, I'll go along with it, but it won't work. There has to be leadership.*

"Instead," Jesus continued, "whoever wants to become great among you must be your servant, and whoever wants to be first must be slave of all."

Now that he didn't like, and Matthew would have said so if he could've gotten a word in edgewise. He'd worked hard to get where he was and there were less able men who could serve as slaves.

So defensive were his thoughts he nearly missed hearing the last of Jesus' conversation. "For even the Son of Man did not come to be served, but to serve, and to give his life as a ransom for many."

*To give his life as a ransom? How am I supposed to understand that,* Matthew fumed, and put it out of his mind.

# 12

# The Burial

JOSEPH TOOK THE BODY, WRAPPED IT IN A CLEAN LINEN
CLOTH, AND PLACED IT IN HIS OWN NEW TOMB . . .
Scripture Reference: Matthew 27:27–66; Mark 15:16–47; Luke 23:25–56; John 19:16–42

Anthony was a third-generation soldier. His father had served as a Legionnaire cavalryman for twenty years, and his grandfather died in the battle of Actium. Anthony began his service patroling various frontiers, but after a few years he moved up in rank to surveyor, then engineer, building walls. Now, billeted in the Tower of Antonia, he was done with camping in the mud and eating poor rations. The mess in the castle was fair and plenty, and his middle grew thicker every day, what with the wine and the leisure Jerusalem afforded.

Ah, the leisure. His men thought it boredom, and perhaps it was for them with only their monotonous gambling games. They missed the sports in other cities. But, as for himself, he enjoyed the pace of Jerusalem with its quaint religious fervor. And he enjoyed his prestige as an officer and admired his appearance in uniform—the crested helmet with scarlet plume, the leather breastplate and wooden shield.

Jerusalem being a Jewish city its people, on the whole, went about their business without incident. On market days there were arguments; feast days were the worst with streets so thronged merchants couldn't get their carts through the gates. In the temple the Jews had skirmishes with their money changers and animal sellers. And the Jews' hatred of Roman authority was never fully placated. Always there was danger of full-fledged revolt, and authorities constantly monitored the temper of the community, fearing an uprising. At feast time every soldier was on duty, instructed to keep a watchful eye and to make Rome's presence known.

Never had a Passover season been more explosive. All week long there had been one uproar after another. Some Galilean fanatic came into the city through the eastern gate riding on an ass with people hailing him as king of the Jews. The ignorant people will believe anything, Anthony had learned, and they looked for any excuse they could find to whip up excitement. The religious leaders were incensed by the whole affair, and one thing led to another.

This self-proclaimed king caused trouble in the temple when he let the animals loose and turned over the tables of the money changers. This ingratiated him to the people and they cheered him on, but it was poor politics. Those of the Jewish establishment were chagrined and furious. Anthony laughed. If the Galilean wanted to be king of the Jews he should have had the good sense to ingratiate himself with those in power, not the fickle people.

There were other incidents during the week concerning the Nazarene, but Anthony had been too busy to learn much about them. If the man had only gone against Jewish traditions he might have been spared his fate, but the Governor couldn't tolerate a king to rival Rome. At last, with all the turmoil and confusion, Pontius Pilate was fed up and turned Jesus over for crucifixion.

As luck would have it Anthony was in charge of the execution squad. There were three criminals to crucify that morning and, frankly, he was glad one of them was a Jew. Executing the Galilean would put the fear of Rome in the Jews. And he was eager to get it over and done with so that Jerusalem could return to normal and he could get some sleep.

Anthony selected men for the detail who were seasoned in the skills of execution. They were older, hardened by the two thousand crucifixions they had carried out in Sepphoris. With that many criminals to execute they had to improvise, nail men to trees, and use the same crosses many times. Working around the clock to get the job done they hastened the deaths by *crucifragium*, breaking the legs of victims.

He often said that if he had his way, he'd use the Assyrian method of execution—impale the body—which was a quicker death than by crucifixion. It would take less time from a soldier's duty. Crucifying could last more than a week.

As he laced on his leg greaves that morning, Anthony whistled a song he'd heard in the street when the pilgrims came into the city. They sang it every Passover and he liked the tune, less like a chant than the others.

Mounting his horse he knew he cut a fine figure and enjoyed the power of authority, the throngs jamming the streets, awed by his presence, parting for his passage. As he rode through the streets more than one young woman caught his eye and then, to his amusement, dropped her flattering gaze. Anthony rode the big roan with pride, its hoofs clattering on the paving stones, its nostrils flared and snorting.

Clear of the crowd he changed the gait to the roan's magnificent canter as the horse and rider passed through the Jaffa gate onto the road below the old water conduit. Outside the city the riotous mob clogged the way, and Anthony used his riding crop to scatter them. Impeded by the crowd he reined the horse off the road and spurred him into a gallop across the ridge.

The centurion drew up at the Place of the Skull where the prisoners were, and the execution squad were readying the timbers and nails. A black man had dragged one of the crosses onto the hill and was resting nearby. Two of the criminals were trembling, sweat streaming down their naked bodies, but the Galilean was too weak to show any sign of fear. The sight of him was revolting; his body bore the marks of the lictor's lash, his flesh so badly lacerated there was little skin left anywhere. On his head was a ridiculous crown of thorns; his hair was blood soaked, his face bruised and swollen. The lips were parched, the eyes sunk in the black holes of their sockets, and patches of his beard had been plucked out by the roots. A soldier tried to wrest the crown from his head but the long thorns were too imbedded. *Ironic*, Anthony thought. *So this is the king of the Jews.*

Some woman caught sight of the crowned one and swooned. Others circled around her wailing, and Anthony watched a youth turn his face away from the Galilean, gagging.

Right away Anthony saw that this was a nasty crowd, some tormentors still spitting on the Jew. They cursed and laughed, gestured obscenely. Apart from the vicious mob the Jew's mourners huddled together—most of them women and one of them, perhaps the man's mother, was supported by a grim young man.

The crowd was parting to let three ranking Pharisees and chief priests through. In their pompousness and finery they looked regal, but Anthony knew that beneath the brilliant mitres and embroidered vestments were cunning minds and treacherous hearts. He gave them ringside positions to witness the execution.

In Jerusalem Jewish women always prepared a drink that deadened the pain for the victims of crucifixion, and now they were handing the potion to a soldier to administer. The elegantly dressed priests watched curiously as the soldier held the drink to one of the criminal's lips. As the frantic man gulped it down they smiled with satisfaction.

The second victim sipped the potion hoping for longer-lasting effect. But the third one, the "king of the Jews," refused the drink, clamping shut his mouth and turning his face away. The soldiers wasted no time coaxing him, but dashed the drug on the ground. Throwing the Jew onto a cross they held him there, stretched his arm flat against the timber, a soldier's knee holding it down, and placed the nail expertly between the bones. Carefully, making sure the nail was aimed just right, the soldier raised his mallet and waited for the order. Anthony steeled himself for the inevitable scream, then gave the word. With one solid stroke, the soldier drove the nail straight through the quivering flesh, but there was no scream! Even as the nail was hammered some more there was no curse—no outcry of any kind!

Anthony pushed the soldiers aside to see if the Jew was dead. He was very much alive, for he was saying something. "Father, forgive them, for they do not know what they are doing."

The soldiers heard him too and didn't know what to make of it. Curious, they looked at the centurion for answer. One of them grinned and shrugged his shoulders. "You get all kinds in this business." Anthony gave the nod and the men proceeded to nail the other arm.

Rifling through the bills of ordinances, Anthony gave them a quick reading. One a thief, a man-stealer for pirates. The other a thief, a highwayman from the Jericho road. The third "Jesus of Nazareth, King of the Jews."

Anthony smiled. The Governor had written the last charge in three languages—Hebrew, Greek, and Latin. *I can just see Pilate gloating over this,* the centurion mused. He had been in the crowd when Pilate stood on the portico and shouted to the riotous mob, "Shall I crucify your king?" and heard the Jews answer back, "We have no king but Caesar." *At last he's made the Jews knuckle under and acknowledge Caesar as their king, something they were loathe to do. As much as they hate Caesar, the words must have stuck in their craw.*

*It's a hard-won victory for Pilate,* Anthony thought, *no wonder he wants to make the most of it.* He read the bill of indictment again, "Jesus of Nazareth, King of the Jews." *What a joke— Pilate's telling the world, "Look what Rome is doing to the king of the Jews!"*

When both of Jesus' arms and feet were affixed, Anthony nailed the bill of ordinances above his head and stood back. His men expertly hoisted the cross and swung it into place, letting it drop with a thud. The jolt must have caused excruciating pain, and the watching women gasped; yet the Jew did not cry out.

Dumbfounded, one of the older soldiers shook his head. "Never seen that before—and him without a potion!"

It was going to be a long day. The week had exhausted the centurion and now that he had to see the executions through to the end, he'd be on duty for days. Anthony went over and unsaddled his horse and let the roan graze on tether. As he returned from tending the horse he heard the thieves cursing, throwing insults along with the crowd. He supposed it diverted attention from themselves. Those executed had various ways of getting through the ordeal. He'd seen men immediately sink into unconsciousness, others go mad from the pain. But the Nazarene disturbed him. *He doesn't react like any other man I've crucified.*

The people, who had been pushing and shoving, vying for the best places to watch the men die, were beginning to settle down. They began eating bread and fruit, taking swigs from wineskins.

Anthony shook his head disgustedly. *I've seen a lot of execution spectators, but never a mob like this. Their high and mighty leaders are as vulgar as the rest.* They taunted the so-called king, shouting, "If you are the Son of God, come down from the cross," and the thieves echoed the challenge. As they kept yelling it over and over, he thought to himself, *I wish they'd shut up! "Son of God, Son of God"—it keeps ringing in my ears.*

When the soldiers' work was done they busied themselves dividing up the clothing of the victims, greedily snatching and grabbing, quarreling for the best.

After a while Anthony noticed that one of the thieves, the highwayman, was quiet, and he studied the man to see if he was so soon unconscious. The cords in his neck stood out like ropes and his teeth chattered from the pain. *He's fevered now,* the centurion thought, *but far from unconscious.* At that moment the man's head turned painfully to one side, and Anthony watched as he gazed upon the would-be king of the Jews.

Mustering strength the highwayman shouted to the other thief, the man-stealer, who was still bellowing insults at the Nazarene, "Don't you fear God since you are under the same sentence?"

Ignoring the question, the man kept on cursing.

The other thief persisted. "We are punished justly, for we are getting what our deeds deserve. But this man has done nothing wrong."

A smirk crossed the man-stealer's lips and he let out a torrent of obscenities.

Anthony found the highwayman's rebuke interesting. A thief would indeed know a crook if he saw one—and by the same token recognize a good man. In fact any fool could see that Jesus of Nazareth was a good man—an extraordinary man.

The thief was saying something more. "Jesus, remember me when you come into your kingdom."

The Nazarene, hanging in that slumped position, hardly had breath to answer him, but in a hoarse voice he made a promise. "I tell you the truth, today you will be with me in paradise."

The Pharisees laughed loud guffaws at that, and Anthony was himself amused. How could any mere man promise such a thing? Then he felt uncomfortable, for ringing in his ears were the words of the taunting Pharisees, "Son of God, Son of God." Trying to shake the disturbing thought, Anthony turned his attention to the soldiers squatting down, busy about something. He leaned over their shoulders to see what they were doing.

The execution squad had divided the victims' clothes into four piles, one for each soldier, but there was an undergarment that was without seam, woven in one piece from top to bottom. "Let's not tear it," one of them said. "Let's decide by lot who gets it." The others agreed and he took out his dice, shook them in his hand, and let them roll.

Anthony was not surprised when the owner of the dice won the robe.

As the morning dragged on, the roan began neighing, tormented by a pack of wild dogs. Anthony left to chase them away and the pack fled as he stoned them. Settling the excited horse, the centurion patted him, spoke soothingly in his ear. He was rubbing the roan's nose when he caught sight of the mourning women. Quickly he looked the other way. He scorned women's tears.

Leaving the horse tethered Anthony returned to the execution. There was so much yelling and laughing going on, he almost missed something the Nazarene was saying. He thought he heard him say, "Dear woman, here is your son." Curious, he followed the direction of the Jew's gaze to a young man on whom the woman leaned. "Here is your mother," Jesus added.

The woman looked up at him but could not bear what she saw. Turning away, she buried her face against the young man's shoulder, and he, comforting her, led her away.

Watching them leave the centurion felt an unusual concern. It was nearly noon and an ominous sensation was creeping up his spine. The sun was darkening by the minute, a deep shade spreading over them, and a feeling of fear pervaded. The crowd grew strangely quiet. The roan skittered about, jerking against the tether; and as the darkness deepened people hastily gathered their things together and began running back to the city. The roan broke the tether, reared on its hind legs, pawed the air, nostrils flared, eyes wild; but before Anthony could get to him the horse plunged to the ground, galloping in stark terror across the field.

The centurion cursed. It was getting too dark to see and his men probably had no torch. As the blackness engulfed them he felt afraid and wanted himself to break and run. Then he saw a torch flare, lighting up the place of execution, and he hurried back to resume his grim duty.

Suddenly the Nazarene uttered an anguished cry, *"Eloi, Eloi, lama sabachthani?"*

Some witnesses standing nearby thought he called for Elijah, but Anthony knew what he said for he knew the Aramaic. "My God, my God, why have you forsaken me?"

Anthony was unnerved by the cry, and taking a torch from the hand of one of the soldiers, he held it up and stared at the Jew, confounded. The dried blood caked to his face all but obscured it from sight; never had he seen a face so marred! In the dancing light of the flame, the tortured body was a bloody pulp, every tendon strained, every nerve burning with pain, yet the man scarcely opened his mouth!

Anthony tried to steady himself by looking away from the crosses, and tried to see the people fleeing. There was a feeble light not far away where that group of women huddled together, reluctant to leave. He admired their courage and wondered at their devotion, although in some measure he was beginning to understand.

No sooner had he calmed himself a bit than the Jew spoke again. "I thirst."

Some fool ran to fill a sponge with wine vinegar. Putting it on a stick, he raised it to the man's cracked lips. Someone laughed and yelled, "Leave him alone, now. Let's see if Elijah comes to take him down."

Of course Elijah did not come, and the Nazarene pressed his lips to the sponge sucking the vinegar as best he could. *He can't last much longer,* Anthony thought.


In a little while Jesus spoke again. "It is finished."

*What's finished?* Anthony asked himself. *Now let's see if he will die. Six hours—he's been hanging there only six hours. That's not long for crucifixion.*

Without warning Jesus regained strength from somewhere and cried out in a loud voice, "Father, into your hands I commit my spirit."

The cry alarmed the soldiers; they gaped in astonishment as Jesus gave a mighty heave, expelling his own life. His head dropped down on his chest and the centurion knew the Jew would not breathe again.

Suddenly the ground beneath their feet moved. A shock wave rumbled under them—then another! People screamed—trees were crashing, boulders bouncing down the hill!

Terrified, Anthony held fast to the swaying cross and cried out to God.

As suddenly as it began the quaking stopped. Too dazed to think, he vaguely heard sounds of bedlam coming from the city. Slowly Anthony realized he must pull himself together. Recovering enough to issue an order to secure the crosses, he eased himself down on the ground.

Still shaken, he told himself he was a brave man but— Looking up at the Jew he had crucified, he felt impelled to say, "Surely he was the Son of God!"

Still dazed, a messenger was tugging at him. "Sir— I say, sir." Pale with fright, the man was desperate to fulfill his mission. "The Jews have a holy day beginning at sundown. It will profane their Sabbath if these men are not dead before then. The priests asked permission of Pilate to have you break their legs, hasten their deaths."

Anthony nodded and motioned to his frightened men. One of them rose unsteadily to his feet. He took a spear in both hands, leveled it crosswise the man-stealer's shins, then struck such a swift blow the leg bones cracked. The body fell forward hanging by the arms alone. Quickly, the chest would fill with fluid and bring on death.

"Leave the Jew for me," Anthony told the soldier, and the man moved to the other thief. The snap of the bones as they cracked signaled a quick death for the poor wretch, and Anthony felt a sense of relief knowing the ordeal would soon be over.

He got up and stood beneath the middle cross holding his spear in his hand. He knew the Nazarene was dead, but he must make sure. Aiming the spear below the rib cage he brought it up with force, ramming it straight up toward the heart. As he yanked it out again, water and blood streamed down from the wound. "Ah!" he heard a soldier exclaim, "He's dead already!"

Anthony cleaned off the spear and stuck it in the ground. Sitting down, he put his head in his hands and waited for the other two to expire. The pack of wild dogs waiting for their feast were restive—barking and leaping up at the dying men. Anthony kicked at them, slapped them with his spear.

No sooner did the thieves breathe their last than the messenger ran back to the city to dispatch the news. Immediately the soldiers set about taking the bodies down from the crosses. Fighting off the dogs, they managed to keep them at bay. First they lifted the cross out of its hole and let it fall to the ground, then they cut the highwayman's limbs free. Throwing the corpse on a litter, two of them took it to the edge of the precipice and dumped it down the hill to the great delight of the yelping dogs. But before they could take down another body, they were interrupted.

Two members of the Sanhedrin, Joseph and Nicodemus, came with an affadavit from Governor Pontius Pilate granting permission for the body of Jesus to be buried. The women who had been standing nearby came closer, trying to hear what was being said.

The soldiers protested. "Look here," one of them said, "transgressors are never buried. It's a rule. We throw their corpses down the side of the hill. Dogs make quick work of them and leave the rest to turkey vultures."

The women shuddered.

"Silence," Anthony ordered, and rolling up the scroll he stuck it in his girdle. It was indeed unusual for an executed man to be buried, but the affadavit seemed genuine, and it was clear these Jews meant business; they'd brought water and a basin for washing the body. He tucked the scroll in his girdle. "How much damage was done in the city?" he asked.

"We had no time to survey the damage," Joseph told him. "You see—"

"We must hasten," Nicodemus interrupted, "Sunset begins our holy Sabbath. Our religion forbids us to bury on a Sabbath."

"In this darkness will you see the sunset?"

"The time is soon," Nicodemus answered.

Noticing that the man brought with him a heavy sack, Anthony asked, "What's that you have there?"

"A hundred pounds of spices, sir. It's our custom to anoint the body—"

Anthony waved him aside. "How well I know. But a *hundred* pounds?"

Nicodemus's voice quavered. "It is little enough for one—"

"Where do you intend to bury this man?"

Joseph spoke up, "There's a garden over there—beneath that ridge. I have a tomb there, one hewn only recently from the rock. It's never been used."

"I see." Joseph also had a sack. "What's in that bag?"

"The linen, sir. See, it's a clean linen cloth to wrap the body in."

Anthony pulled out the scroll again, mulled over it, then addressed his men. "Help them take down the body—the one in the middle—that one. The King of the Jews."

Soldiers lowered the cross, but Joseph and Nicodemus undertook the task of disengaging the feet and arms from the nails. It was difficult, and the crown of thorns was so imbedded Anthony told them, "I don't think you can remove it."

Unable to take the pains they would like because of the Sabbath coming on, the men bathed the body quickly and poured on myrrh and aloes ointments. Wrapping the corpse in the long strips of linen, they bound limbs to the body and covered the head with a napkin. Laying the body on a litter, with a man at either end of it they carried it away.

Anthony watched the men and women making their toilsome way and he felt an urge to follow them. He, too, felt bent over with the burden of the body and profound grief. But he dare not give in to such feelings.

Instead he swatted at the flies and proceeded to oversee the stacking of the crosses for another round of executions. Never before had a crucifixion affected him as this one. *But then again, there's never been a man like the one we crucified today. Surely he was the Son of God.*

That night after a few hours rest—for he could not sleep—Anthony hoped the day would bring relief, but before he had shaved the Governor sent for him. The chief priests and Pharisees were worried and went to Pilate about their concern. "Sir," they said, "we remember that while he was still alive that deceiver said, 'After three days I will rise again.' So give us the order for the tomb to be made secure until the third day. Otherwise his disciples may come and steal the body and tell the people that he has been raised from the dead. This last deception will be worse than the first."

Pilate told them to make the tomb as secure as they could and left it up to Anthony to take care of the matter. Anthony led the Jews to the garden where they saw the tomb in the side of the hill with a stone rolled before its mouth. Tracks in the fresh earth showed signs of the recent activity, and there was the scent of incense about.

While a Legionnaire prepared a pot of clay, Anthony carefully removed the Roman seal from his pouch and rubbed it with his hand. The chief priests eyed his every move. A cord was stretched across the stone and affixed on either side. Then a lump of clay was softened and a glob of it pressed against either end of the cord. With the insignia Anthony imprinted the seal of Rome onto the clay. Even a child could break the seal, but no one would dare, for to break the seal of Rome brought the death penalty by torture and crucifixion. The contents of the tomb were as secure as man could make them.

The chief priests examined his work and were satisfied.

"You're to set quarternions of soldiers to guard this tomb every minute, day and night," one of them said.

"It's been done," Anthony answered, feeling nothing but contempt for them. Under his breath he said, "He was the Son of God," and he did not care that they heard him.

# 13

# Mary Magdalene

THEY HAVE TAKEN MY LORD AWAY AND I DON'T
KNOW WHERE THEY HAVE PUT HIM.

Scripture Reference: Matthew 28:1–15; Mark 16:1–11;

Luke 24:1–12; John 20:1–18

The sweet scent of myrrh filled the house where the women were working. Mary, the mother of James, and Salome let the beans pour through their fingers into the mortar as Mary Magdalene turned the pestle, crushing them against the sides. Mary Magdalene mingled her tears with the spices, mourning the death of Jesus. Other women were helping, washing vessels, filling jars—the wife of Zebedee, Joanna, the wife of Cuza, Susanna, and several others—women who had followed Jesus, ministering to his needs. Some of them were sleeping from exhaustion such as only grief can cause. From the hour he was arrested, they had clung to each other, praying, weeping the long night through. Then, when the verdict was finally given, they took off their ornaments, threw dust on their heads, and gave vent to grief.

Along the street, on their way to Golgotha, they had encountered other weeping women to whom Jesus had just spoken, telling them to weep for themselves and their children. Mary Magdalene was not clear about all he said.

Steeling themselves, the women resolved not to desert him during the ordeal although every blow, every pain he bore intensified their anguish. Standing as close to the cross as they were allowed, they watched in abject horror as the soldiers tortured him, the religious leaders shouting indignities, the basest of men abusing him. All day long mangey dogs bayed about the crosses, yapping, yapping at him, as if they sensed the animal mood of the persecutors and knew they had license.

The agony was more than Mary Magdalene could bear. To look upon his dear face, battered and bloody, the beard half plucked away, his naked body cut to ribbons, his limbs stretched taut, blood streaming down; to hear his groans was unbearable.

For hours they waited. An awesome darkness rolled over the noonday sun causing people to run helter skelter, but it only made the women cling to each other, determined to stay by the Lord until the end.

Numb with grief, they endured the long hours until at last they heard Jesus shouting, his words splitting the skies! "Father, into your hands I commend my spirit."

At that very moment a loud rumbling shook the earth beneath their feet! The women were knocked off their feet. Rocks split in two—stones sealing tombs fell away!

But, as suddenly as it began, the earthquake stopped. Shaken, Mary Magdalene struggled to her feet and looked about. The centurion looked panic-stricken, then she heard him say, "Surely, he was the Son of God!"

In a few minutes, recovering from the shock, the centurion glanced at his men and motioned for them to continue. They steadied the crosses, saw that the bodies were securely fastened.

"I think our Lord is dead," Susannah said.

Mary Magdalene studied his form hanging there and saw no sign of life.

After a while, on the order of the centurion, the soldiers began breaking the legs of the men on the crosses. Mary Magdalene, still trembling from head to foot, could not watch. Her face buried in her lap, she heard the snap of bones as first one, then another bone was broken. Listening for the third pair of legs to break, she waited. Still terrified, Susanna and the other Mary began whispering. *It must be all over,* Mary Magdalene thought, and raised her eyes. Just at that moment the centurion rammed a spear into Jesus' body. Joanna's face whitened and she eased down on the ground beside Mary. "He's dead," someone said softly.

There were no tears left in the women; Mary felt release; the ordeal was over.

Right away soldiers began taking down one of the crosses, and the dogs were in a frenzy, leaping up, barking, dancing about. Mary Magdalene felt she would go mad if she allowed herself to think about his body being dumped down the hill to be devoured by those dogs.

"It's not the body of Jesus," Joanna told her.

As the soldiers hauled the corpse to the edge of the precipice the dogs were alongside, yelping and leaping up to drag the body from the litter.

About that time the women noticed two men who had come out from the city. As they stood talking with the centurion the women tried to see who they were. "One of them looks like Joseph from Arimathea," Susannah said. "He's a member of the Sanhedrin."

"The other one's Nicodemus. I'd know him anywhere," Joanna said. "He's on the Sanhedrin, too."

Mary Magdalene bit her knuckle so as not to cry out! As the men were talking, the soldiers were lowering the cross on which the Lord was hung. Her heart beat rapidly, fearing what would come next. But when the cross was laid flat on the ground the soldiers stood aside while Joseph and Nicodemus knelt down beside Jesus' body. "What are they doing?" someone asked, and the women moved in closer. "Could it be that they have permission to bury Jesus?" Mary asked.

"Perhaps, but where?"

When they were near enough they saw that Joseph and Nicodemus were unfastening the arms of Jesus from the nails. His limbs were stiff, his flesh looked bloodless, as white and cold as marble. Mary Magdalene could not look. "Tell me when they're done."

Not until the men had bathed the body, hurriedly anointed

it with spices, and wrapped it in grave clothes did Joanna touch Mary's sleeve. "Come, let's go with them," she said. The men were lifting the body onto a bier and the women offered to help. Joseph waved them aside, lifted his end of the litter as Nicodemus took the other end, and led the way downhill. The women following alongside quickened their step to keep up with the men.

"We have burial spices for him," Mary Magdalene told Joseph. "We have them in the city, but they're not prepared yet."

"There's no time now," Nicodemus told her, and lifted his head toward the horizon where the sinking sun spread a narrow band of gold across the sky.

Reaching the path leading down the hill they went single file, and by climbing down and around they came to the tomb where the body was to be laid.

It was a new tomb, dug out of the limestone side of the hill, and faced west where the setting sun signaled the fast approach of the high holy day of Passover. They scarcely had time to position the body on the narrow shelf before the day would be over and the Sabbath begun.

Backing out of the tomb, the two men straightened up and shook their heads sadly. "We really didn't finish," Joseph said, and put his shoulder to the stone to roll it before the door of the tomb. "The work isn't finished, but as you can see anything more must wait until after the Sabbath."

The women discussed among themselves what they might do. "We'll prepare the spices and as soon as the Sabbath ends, come here early on the first day."

The women stayed on at the tomb watching the men as they worked to roll the round wheel of a stone before the mouth of the cave. Just as it was settled into place the last tip of the sun sank behind the horizon and the *shofar* sounded from the wall of the city. Joseph and Nicodemus brushed dirt from their hands, bid the women farewell, and started back to Jerusalem.

The Seder would begin after sundown and although the women had no heart for it, they felt it their duty to help John Mark's mother serve the roasted lamb, unleavened bread, and bitter herbs. Wrapping the bread in a napkin, Mary Magdalene's tears fell on the table. Joanna, lighting the lamps, observed her distress. "Leave that," she said. "I'll take care of it. Go, Mary. I'll pour the wine."

Mary, the mother of Jesus was in seclusion in an upstairs room, and when Mary Magdalene could no longer stand suffering alone she decided to join Mary. She was slipping up the outside steps leading to Mary's room when she heard a young boy's voice asking, "Why is this night of Passover different from all other nights of the year?"

The words stabbed her forcibly, anguished as she was by the events of that day. It was as if the question applied to her own aching heart for, to be sure, there would never be another night like this one; a night in which her fondest hopes were dashed, her bitterest memory forged. She sat down on the steps, put her head on her knees and sobbed.

In her misery she could not shut out the cruelities inflicted on Jesus. The sight of his broken, bleeding body was ever before her, the sound of the crowd's bloodthirsty cry, "Crucify him! Crucify him!" rang in her ears.

So anguished was she, she had no room for fear even though there was reason to be terrified. Of the disciples, only John was anywhere about; the others were hiding out and soon John would join them. Mary Magdalene wondered if they might all be put to death and, dispirited as she was, that prospect was not unwelcome. *Must we all flee?* she wondered. *But where?*

All night long she sat on the step, sleepless and despairing. *Even if all goes well and the authorities don't persecute us, what will we do? Return to the old ways?* The thought of doing so repelled her. *Impossible, I will never go back!*

As the sun rose the next morning she got up from the stair stiff and sore. It was the first day of the Feast of Unleavened Bread and a Sabbath marked the beginning of that holy week. Mary Magdalene had no heart for Sabbath day observance but all day long she obediently conformed going through the motions of all the obligations.

Finally, when the sun was setting, she took a seat by the window and waited for the moon to rise.

As the moon rose and took its long journey up and across the night sky, pilgrims camping outside the city sang psalms around their campfires; and Mary Magdalene, listening, reflected on her past life before she met Jesus. Even as a child growing up in the village of Magdala, she had been tormented by demons. Meeting Jesus delivered her, and now for more than a year she had been free from any visitation by the seven evil spirits. Such freedom she had never known before. But with Jesus dead she did not like to think what might happen. *Will the demons come back?* she wondered.

As the night wore on and the moon waned, hanging low and lopsided above the horizon, she began to feel afraid. *What will happen to us?*

In time weariness overwhelmed her, and she stretched out on the floor hoping to sleep. The hours dragged by and sleep never came.

The next day was the regular seventh day Sabbath. Two Sabbaths in succession seemed intolerable to the women who wanted most of all to get to the tomb, apply their ointments and sweet-smelling unctions to the body of Jesus.

Already the city was returning to normal after Passover, the religious leaders strutting about, euphoric over their victory. Still the women had to wait before they could prepare the spices and return to the grave. Anxiety like a contagion spread among them.

When darkness finally fell again and the Sabbath ended, Mary Magdalene and the other Mary took down the mortar, the pestle, and the beans containing myrrh. As they worked fragrances filled the house. Joanna and the others washed containers, filled and sealed them securely. They worked for some time until all the spices were prepared, then laid down again to await the dawn.

They had hardly dozed when noises awakened them. They felt the house shake—not once, but twice, upsetting a stool and rattling crockery on a shelf. "Another tremor," Joanna said, and Mary Magdalene jumped up and ran to the door. The moon was clouded over and the sky looked threatening. Mary and Susanna were looking over her shoulder. "Do you think it's over?" Mary Magdalene asked.

"Whether or not it is, let's go," Susannah whispered, "I can't wait any longer."

"Nor I," Joanna confessed, and the others agreed.

Slipping down one street after another, they threaded their way through excited pilgrims and Roman guards, their scarlet tunics visible in the light of their torches. Shouts and curses filled the air, but few people seemed injured in any way. A collapsed roof lay as rubble inside the walls of a stall, and a rabbi was helping a frantic tailor salvage his possessions. Here and there fires blazed, and water brigades were falling into place. A merchant with a lantern was running about wildly—stumbling over paving stones uprooted by the quake. Sheep and goats were bleating, running amuck, and in the midst of it all a noisy horse cart clattered past the women, a farmer bringing live chickens to market.

Anxious to escape the confusion the women hurried through the gate. Walking outside in the open country Susanna asked Mary Magdalene, "Who will roll the stone away from the entrance to the tomb?"

Mary shook her head and, thinking to herself, she wondered if they could pry it away—use a stout limb for leverage.

"If only it were daylight!" Mary exclaimed. The way was littered with cast-offs left by the crowd fleeing the crucifixion three days before—a scarf here, a sandal there.

As the women hurried along daybreak was loath to cast the first color in the sky—the night lingering as if brooding over the darksome days just past.

They were rounding the hill now, descending, and Mary Magdalene shifted the sack of incense from her shoulder to her hip.

The women ahead of her suddenly stopped dead in their tracks. Mary Magdalene gasped! The stone was rolled away and two men in clothes that shone like lightning were standing beside Joanna and Susannah. Quaking from head to toe the women bowed down, their faces to the ground. The men told them not to fear. "Why do you look for the living among the dead? He is not here; he has risen!"

Mary could feel her heart thumping in her chest as one of the men spoke. "Remember how he told you, while he was still with you in Galilee, 'The Son of Man must be delivered into the hands of sinful men, be crucified and on the third day be raised again.' "

Her head spinning, Mary Magdalene stared, the words coming back to her like an echo from the past.

"Come and see the place where he lay," he told them.

Trembling, they took a step forward, peered inside trying to see. When their eyes grew accustomed to the dark they saw a young man sitting on the right side in a white garment. "Don't be alarmed," he said. "You are looking for Jesus the Nazarene, who was crucified. He has risen! He is not here. See the place where they laid him."

Their hands shaking, the women examined the shelf where the body had been laid. It was empty except for the grave clothes lying there.

Then the man told them, "Go, tell his disciples and Peter,

'He is going ahead of you into Galilee. There you will see him, just as he told you.' "

Bewildered, the women backed outside again. For a moment they hesitated, fear and joy exciting them. Then they scrambled back up the hill and ran for the city.

All talking at once, the women excitedly told the disciples what they had seen, but the men were very skeptical. The women listened as Nathanael, Thomas, James, and Simon Peter discussed it among themselves. "Idle tales," one of them said. "Women get distraught, you know." He turned his back. "It's the strain, you know. Women are affected by these things more than we. They're simply beside themselves. Tell them to go home and rest."

Their reception of the women's news had a sobering effect upon Mary Magdalene as well as the others. Although the women told them word for word what was said and all that had happened, when the men did not believe them, the women themselves began to doubt.

"Nonsense," the disciples said. And, so sure the women were hysterical, they did not question them further but resumed their gloomy vigil.

Only Peter and John showed any interest at all. "You say he said 'and Peter'?" Simon Peter asked. The women assured him this was so. Peter got up, unbolted the door, and left the room. John went after him to go to the tomb.

In a few minutes the women followed. Closing the door behind them, they heard the bolt inside being locked in place. Wearily, they went down the stairs leading to the street. The moon had sunk below the horizon, leaving only the stars appearing. "What shall we do?" they wondered aloud.

Mary Magdalene was troubled. No doubt the men were right about the strain being too much for them. She knew that she, for one, in such distress might well have taken leave of her senses. She decided to go back to the tomb, and as she went she reproached herself. *Who indeed is Mary of Magdala to think she saw* angels? *The irony of imagining such a thing—Mary of Magdala, familiar with evil spirits, seven to be exact. Certainly no angel would appear to me.*

The reasoning brought on a bitter gloom, and Mary turned her thoughts to consider where the body might be. If anything, she reasoned, it was stolen—carried away and dumped some place.

An emaciated dog appeared in the way, barring its teeth, growling at her. She picked up a rock and hurled it. The dog tucked its tail and ran off in the darkness.

*Oh, what if the dogs somehow got to him?* she fretted.

She glanced over her shoulder to see if the other women were coming, but she didn't see them. *If only the sun would rise! It would burn away the heavy mist, and with daylight I could see better. If only the body is in the tomb*—she hoped desperately, fighting back the tears. *If the body isn't there, I'll search for him until I find him, and somehow, some way, I'll see that he is buried.*

Cautiously she descended the incline, feeling for footholds, and from below she could hear voices. Once on the level ground of the garden she saw Peter and John coming out of the tomb. From the grave looks on their faces, she knew the body was not there. Preoccupied, they scarcely noticed her as they passed her in the darkness.

Mary Magdalene approached the gaping hole of the cave where a soldier's helmet lay on the ground. She rolled it over with the toe of her sandle and let it lay. Something about the helmet triggered a fresh flood of tears, and as she wept, she leaned down and looked inside the tomb. What she saw startled her. Two angels in white were seated where Jesus' body had been, one at the head and the other at the foot! Before she could recover, they asked her, "Woman, why are you crying?"

Before she answered she searched the tomb. There was no body in the tomb—only the linen wrappings and the napkin that had been about his face lying folded neatly in a place by itself.

"They have taken my Lord away," she answered, choking back the tears, "and I don't know where they have put him." Some movement behind her distracted Mary, and she turned around to see a man standing a little distance away.

"Woman, why are you crying?" he asked. "Who is it you are looking for?"

*He's the gardener,* she thought, and turned back to the tomb. *Maybe he knows*—"Sir, if you have carried him away, tell me where you have put him, and I will get him."

There was a lengthy pause, then the man spoke her name! "Mary."

Suddenly she recognized the voice and wheeled around. *It's the Lord!* "Teacher!" she cried out, and running to him fell at his feet. Wrapping her arms around his ankles she clung to him.

"Do not hold on to me, for I have not yet returned to the Father."

Reluctantly, Mary let go of him then stood up and gazed upon him.

"Go instead to my brothers and tell them, 'I am returning to my Father and to your Father, to my God and your God.'"

Mary, her heart racing, backed away from him, staring in utter astonishment. Then she turned and ran as fast as she could to tell the disciples.

# 14

# The Vacant Tomb

HE SAW AND BELIEVED.

Scripture Reference: John 20:1–10; Luke 24:12

J ohn was the younger of the two, which explained his ability to run faster, but there was nothing slow about Simon Peter either. When the women told them the grave was empty and that angels were down there the two disciples wasted no time—not that they believed the women—but to set the record straight, to squelch any wild rumors that might come of it.

John reached the tomb in record time; breathless and taken aback by what he saw, he waited for Simon to come. Sure enough, the stone was jarred loose from the grave and rolled a few feet away—probably by the quake, he thought. And there were no soldiers about to tell what happened—nor angels, for that matter—not that he expected any. Angels, that is.

John leaned over to peer inside the cave. If he expected anything it was to see the body swathed in linen or the remains of it left by wild animals. In the predawn darkness it was hard to see inside, so he lit the torch he had brought. In the light every nook and cranny were plain to see, and there was no body lying on the shelf. He saw the strips of linen lying there, as well as the burial cloth that had been around Jesus' head. The cloth was folded up by itself, separate from the linen.

There were no signs of scuffle, of disarray, and the orderliness of it struck John as intentional. Being younger he feared to express his opinion before Simon Peter had a look. Hearing him coming, John stood aside to give him room. Peter brushed past him and, ducking his head, rushed inside the tomb. Cautiously, John followed him. What he saw convinced him that Jesus was alive!

Without a word Simon Peter led the way outside. The two of them did not linger in the garden but climbed the steep path to go back to the city. When they reached level ground and he had given Simon Peter time enough to speak, John decided to go ahead of him and let Simon walk alone with his thoughts.

Reason told him that Simon wasn't sure of himself, not since denying Jesus at the trial. John shook his head remorsefully. *How much I wish we'd both been brave enough to stand by Jesus' side at that trial. If we had insisted, perhaps the Sanhedrin would have let us defend him.* He chided himself, *I could have done it . . . I could have given witness, but I didn't!* Then he rationalized, *We wouldn't have turned the tide. They were determined to kill him.*

Still, John regretted his silence as much as Simon his swearing denials. When the women came from the tomb and told Simon the angel had said they should tell the disciples "and Peter," he saw Simon's surprise and John was glad for him. It meant Jesus held no grudge. *If he does not hold Peter's denial against him,* John reasoned, *no doubt he's forgiven me as well.*

John remembered that on the way to the tomb they had feared raising their hopes, knowing how hysterical women can be, but now that they had seen the tomb, John knew one thing—robbers had not stolen the body. Robbers would never take the time to remove the winding sheet nor to fold the napkin and leave it lying neatly. There was no sign of struggle, nothing to suggest that wild animals had been there.

As for angels, well, there were none, only an empty tomb—but that was enough for him. A great surge of hope rose in him and John quickened his pace anxious to find out what the others would make of this. He looked back over his shoulder to see if Peter were coming. Far behind he saw Peter standing, talking with someone. John couldn't see who the other person was, he could only make out that he was a man.

*Well,* he decided, *I'll not wait for him. Mary must hear this and the Twelve. Even if they don't think Jesus is alive, at least it will cheer them to know the body was not stolen nor eaten by wild animals.*

# 15

# The Emmaus Couple

JESUS HIMSELF CAME UP AND WALKED ALONG WITH THEM.
Scripture Reference: Luke 24:13–48; Mark 16:12–13; John 20:19–25

It was all very disturbing, and when the other pilgrims packed up to leave the city, Cleopas told his wife they were going home too. They were walking the seven miles to Emmaus, and perhaps by the time they arrived home his wife would calm down. Cleopas had just told her about the report of the guards, how they were telling everyone Jesus' disciples had stolen the body while they slept.

"That's a poor lie, Cleopas. If they were asleep how can they be so certain his disciples stole the body?"

She had a point.

"You know those priests, they're not above bribing the guards to get them to say anything they want them to."

He wanted to believe it was a lie, yet there was no reasonable explanation for believing the corpse of Jesus was alive. He shook his head.

"Think about it, Cleopas," she argued, "would a Roman soldier admit to sleeping on guard duty?"

He didn't answer, not wanting to encourage her. She was almost beside herself as it was and couldn't stop talking about it. "Husband, I wish you weren't in such a hurry to get home. I'd like to get to the bottom of this. I know you don't believe my friends, but when they told me they saw Jesus, I believed them."

"You must admit they're high strung, and what we've been

through this past week is enough to make them imagine anything."

"You men are all alike."

Cleopas didn't want her angry. "Well, dear, it is a bit much to think they met a corpse who greeted them."

"They held him by the feet, worshiped him." Her voice was getting shrill. "Do you think they'd worship a corpse?"

"Tell me again what he said."

"He told them to tell his disciples to go to Galilee, that he'd meet them there." Her voice was softer, as if she was not quite so sure; self-conscious that what she was saying sounded ridiculous.

Cleopas stroked his beard. "What about the other—do you believe that too?"

"You mean about the graves being opened and the dead coming back?"

"Yes. Didn't the women say the earthquake caused the tombs to break open—"

"That much I believe."

"But the other—the holy dead walking the streets of Jerusalem—do you believe that too?"

Her face clouded. "A lot of people claim they saw them."

Cleopas heaved a sigh. He felt more fear than hope and his poor wife was so vexed she would not let the matter rest.

A stranger overtook them, and drawing alongside he walked with them. "What are you discussing together as you walk along?" he asked.

They stopped in the middle of the road, surprised that he would ask such a question—the whole city was buzzing with the events of the past few days. "Are you the only one living in Jerusalem who doesn't know the things that have happened there in these days?"

"What things?" the stranger asked.

"About Jesus of Nazareth," they both said at once.

They resumed their journey, walking slowly as Cleopas

explained. "He was a prophet, powerful in word and deed before God and all the people. The chief priests and our rulers handed him over to be sentenced to death, and they crucified him; but we had hoped that he was the one who was going to redeem Israel. And what is more, it is the third day since all this took place. In addition, some of our women amazed us. They went to the tomb early this morning but didn't find his body. They came and told us that they had seen a vision of angels, who said he was alive. Then some of our companions went to the tomb and found it just as the women had said, but him they did not see."

The stranger seemed displeased. "How foolish you are, and how slow of heart to believe all that the prophets have spoken! Did not the Christ have to suffer these things and then enter his glory?"

Cleopas felt rebuked, but the man went on to explain. He began at the books of the Law and went straight through the scriptures explaining the prophecies relating to the Messiah. What a scholar he was! From the Psalms, Isaiah, and Daniel he showed them that the Messiah must be wounded, chastised, "cut off." As he talked, all they could think of were the remarkable parallels in the sufferings of Jesus.

As they listened, Cleopas and his wife exchanged glances, excited by what they were hearing. What this stranger was saying made sense!

As the three approached the village, engrossed as they were, they walked even slower, not wanting the conversation to end. There was a fork in the road and the stranger was breaking off the conversation to go north. Cleopas's wife protested, "Oh, no," she said, "come home with us."

"Please, you must," Cleopas insisted. "Stay with us, for it's nearly evening; the day is almost over."

So, the stranger consented and went home with them.

Inside the house Cleopas and their guest sat down before the table waiting for supper. Quickly the woman set bread and mutton before them and paused to hear the blessing. The guest took the bread, gave thanks to God, then broke it, and passed it to Cleopas.

A strange awareness was taking place. Cleopas looked at his wife to see if. . . . Simultaneously it was happening! As if scales fell from their eyes, recognition dawned on them. Their guest was Jesus!

Cleopas turned to look at him again. But he was gone! Vanished!

Cleopas stared at his wife and she at him. Finding his voice, he whispered, "Were not our hearts burning within us while he talked with us on the road and opened the scriptures to us?"

"Yes! Yes!" she agreed ecstatically.

Cleopas jumped up knocking over a bench. "Come, let's go back to Jerusalem. We've got to tell them!"

# 16

# The Ghost

DO YOU HAVE ANYTHING HERE TO EAT?

Scripture Reference: Luke 24:36–49; John 20:19–25

J ohn sighed and pushed his plate aside, the fish half eaten. He worried about the lock on the one door. If two strong men put their weight against it, the bolt would give. After all, the women were with them, and ten men could hardly protect them from a mob. In the street below there was an ugly mood among the people standing about. As he and Simon Peter returned from the tomb, they had passed close by a group of potters, and John could feel the hostility even before they began spitting curses. The danger was real, and if the men and women gathered in that upper room knew what was good for them, they'd hurry up and decide on an escape plan.

Andrew fingered the jar of honey and stared unseeing. In his mind he visualized Judas dangling from the tree, the rope breaking, his body dashed below on the rocks. Bitterly he thought to himself, *How could I have been such a fool as to be taken in by that man!*

Philip stood by the narrow window watching the street below. Thomas should be coming any minute now. A knot of angry Jews stood on the corner, their torches casting grotesque shadows on the walls. The agitation he felt was almost too much to bear. When the women came with their story of having seen the Lord, he had not been impressed; but now that Simon had seen Jesus, Philip was confused and nervous.

Two people were half-running down the street—half-running, as if they were tired or did not want to attract attention. As they came nearer Philip recognized Cleopas and his wife. "Cleopas is coming," he announced, and got ready to unlock the door. He could hear them on the steps. Unbolting the door, he opened it, and they burst in the room.

Philip didn't give them a chance to say anything so anxious was he to tell them, "The Lord has risen and has appeared to Simon."

"We know," the woman said, wide-eyed with excitement. "We saw him!"

"You *saw* him? Who?"

"Jesus. We saw him—talked with him."

People in the room rushed to hear. "Where?" "When?" they wanted to know.

Cleopas explained, "We were on our way home, talking about all the things that have happened, when this stranger drew alongside."

"Stranger?"

"Well, yes, at first. We didn't recognize him until later."

"Oh?" they said, questioning the credibility of such a story. Several were exchanging knowing glances.

Cleopas was frantic to regain their confidence. "Hear me out!" They made room for him to sit down. He continued. "He—the stranger, I mean—asked why we were troubled and we told him. We explained how we had hoped Jesus would redeem Israel, but instead the authorities had taken him and crucified him. We told him how these women here went to the tomb this morning and came back saying the body was gone.

"After we told him all that, he scolded us for being slow to believe what the prophets have said. Then as we walked along together, he began explaining from the scriptures how it was prophesied that the Messiah should suffer and die and be raised again."

His wife interrupted. "We knew right away that what he was saying was true."

"Oh, yes, it all rang true. But we didn't realize who he was until we reached Emmaus. He made as if he would leave us and go on alone, but we persuaded him to come home with us."

"You didn't recognize him?" Matthew asked.

"Not right away," the wife said. "I served supper and when this 'stranger' gave thanks, he broke the bread and passed it to Cleopas. Suddenly our eyes were opened and we recognized that he was Jesus!"

"Your eyes were opened?"

"I can't explain it—I think a veil came between—something like that."

"What happened then?" Philip asked.

Cleopas hesitated, glanced about at them as if he was afraid to say. Then he spoke softly. "He disappeared—just vanished from sight—"

The disciples looked at one another, mystified. "Disappeared?" someone repeated. And by the way he said it he sounded skeptical.

For a long time there was little more than scepticism in the room, each person pondering all he had heard, trying to understand, wanting to believe but not daring to believe. As the evening wore on their consternation became more and more apparent. The very real threat of violence on the street below counteracted any hope they might entertain; at best they were bewildered.

Suddenly there was a stir in the middle of the room. Those who were reclining at the table sat up, frightened by what they were seeing. Philip craned his neck to see over John's head. Before them stood the ghost of Jesus!

He spoke. "Why are you troubled, and why do doubts rise in your minds?"

Philip was so frightened he held on to John, afraid he might pass out.

Then, to their amazement, he said, "Look at my hands and my feet." He was lifting the skirt of his robe showing the wounds in his feet. "It is I myself!" he assured them. "Touch me and see; a ghost does not have flesh and bones, as you see I have."

At his insistence, Philip, along with others, felt of his arm— the flesh warm to the touch, the muscle and bone of it firm.

Then Jesus held out his hands and going around the room he showed the nail wounds to each of them.

Philip's heart was racing. It was too good to be true!

"Do you have anything here to eat?" Jesus asked.

There was a piece of fish on a plate in front of John. He handed it to Andrew to pass along. They passed the plate from hand to hand until it reached the nail-riven hand. Jesus, reclining on one of the couches before the table, pulled the flesh from the bones and began eating the fish.

"This is what I told you," he said, "while I was still with you. Everything must be fulfilled that is written about me in the Law of Moses, the Prophets, and the Psalms.

He talked then for a while, explaining scripture after scripture. "This is what is written: The Christ will suffer and rise from the dead on the third day, and repentance and forgiveness of sins will be preached in his name to all nations, beginning at Jerusalem."

Philip was beginning to understand and as he looked at the others, they, too, seemed to grasp what Jesus was saying.

Jesus stood up again, "Peace be with you! As the Father has sent me, I am sending you."

Then he breathed on them and said, "Receive the Holy

Spirit. If you forgive anyone his sins, they are forgiven; if you do not forgive them, they are not forgiven."

As quietly and as mysteriously as he had appeared, he left.

The shock of Jesus' appearance did not wear off immediately, but when it did joy exploded in the room! Women embraced one another weeping; men shouted ecstatic praises to God!

In the midst of the commotion there came a knock on the door, and Philip peeped out to see Thomas standing there. He unbolted the lock, and as Thomas came inside the disciples rushed to tell him what had happened.

Thomas, shaking his head in disbelief, waved them aside and made his way to the table. They were all talking at once trying to convince him but Thomas kept shaking his head. He motioned to one of the women that he'd like some food and wearily sat down.

The bombardment continued, and Thomas nodded, assuring them he heard them, but obviously did not believe what they were saying.

Finally he got them to be quiet for a minute. Then he told them emphatically, "Unless I see the nail marks in his hands and put my finger where the nails were, and put my hand into his side, I will not believe it." For a moment the room was quiet.

The woman served him fish and a honeycomb and he set about eating it. Then the room exploded again. "We saw his hands, his feet!" "I felt his arm!" Philip shouted, "It was the arm of a man, not a ghost!"

"Only an apparition," he answered cooly as he separated the bones from the fish.

The woman who had served Thomas held up the empty plate with the fish bones Jesus had left. "Thomas," she said, "he ate fish the same as you're eating. Don't tell me a ghost can eat!"

With a mouthful bulging his cheek, Thomas signaled time out to swallow. Then he told them again, "Unless I see the nail marks in his hands and put my finger where the nails were, and put my hand into his side, I will not believe it."

# 17

# Thomas

MY LORD AND MY GOD!

Scripture Reference: John 20:24–29

The first day of the week ended and the second began; expectantly the disciples and the women waited for Jesus to appear again. But the morning passed and at noon Thomas raised his eyebrows as much as to say, "Well, where is he?"

The disciples smiled good-naturedly, confident Jesus would come at any moment. So sure were they that they did not want to leave the room for fear they'd miss him. Nor did they dare for fear of enemies in the city. They whiled away the afternoon and speculated that he would come in the evening when they were eating again, or shortly afterward, as he had the night before.

But he didn't. They sat up late waiting, still he did not come.

In the morning Thomas's confirmed opinion was reinforced further when there was no sign of Jesus; and though his conviction gave Thomas no pleasure, there was the satisfaction of knowing he had not gone overboard. He felt betrayed, disillusioned by the whole affair—so much so he had no heart for saying, "I told you so."

When the third day came and went, Thomas was ready to risk leaving their company—if perchance he might find solace elsewhere, but they insisted that he stay still believing Jesus would reappear.

It was raining, and as he looked out the narrow window the pain of his sorrow was as acute as it had been the week before.

On that same night one week before he had sat across from Jesus and heard him say the cup was his blood and the bread his broken body. He had not understood then and he didn't understand now.

Thomas drew in his breath and the heaviness inside him was like a sodden sack of meal. Fragments of things Jesus had told them during that last supper were coming back to him. Jesus had said something about Simon Peter denying him, and what he said had come true. Thomas shook his head. Now Peter was claiming that Jesus had appeared to him. It didn't add up. After such denial, how could Peter make anyone believe that Jesus, if he was alive, sought him out?

The rain pelted on the pavement below, and he watched children splashing barefoot in the run-off. He thought about the other thing Jesus said that was so remarkably fulfilled, the prediction that one of them would betray him. If there was one man among them whom they all trusted, it was Judas Iscariot. That night in Gethsemane Thomas hadn't given it a thought that Judas was not with them. So tired he fell asleep right away, Thomas remembered waking up in the nick of time as the mob was coming through the garden. He had raced to Jesus' side and even when he saw Judas stepping forward from the mob, he didn't realize what Judas was up to.

The more he thought about it, the more he realized that it was a miracle they hadn't all been arrested. *Yes,* he thought ironically, *a miracle.*

The room was stuffy with so many people milling about. They were becoming quieter, and Thomas wondered if they, too, were torturing themselves with thoughts of what had happened on this day a week ago.

The rain stopped in the early evening, and some of those assembled in the room slipped outside to get fresh air and to attend their various duties. The women stayed on with John and some of the others, still adamant about having seen Jesus. Thomas shook his head, wishing they would give up—let the matter rest.

On the fourth day Thomas knew they were remembering the crucifixion. He could see it in their eyes, sense it in their hushed voices, the wretched memory tormenting them. None dare speak of it lest they lose control, but the women wept quietly and comforted each other. As noon drew on he thought of the terrible darkness that had covered them, the quaking of the earth.

"It's been four days, perhaps we're not to see him again?" one of the women said.

No one answered. Thomas knew then they had lost hope that they would see Jesus again, yet they were steadfast about having seen him since his death. Thomas had only to broach the subject but what they all flew at him at once, insisting that Jesus was alive and repeating the same stories about where he'd been seen and by whom. It made his head reel.

The next day dawned early, and Thomas sank deeper in despair as he remembered the day of Passover the week before. That day was marked by a blackness of soul he would never forget—his master brutalized, nothing but a mangled corpse half-way buried in another man's grave. That evening, too grief-stricken to fear anything, he had walked alone to the Temple to lose himself in the hustle and bustle of the pilgrim crowds. The torn curtain had not been repaired, and he was told that temporary screens had been placed before it lest some inquisitive eye gaze upon the Holiest of Holies. At the time he had a great urge to dash through the Holy Place and rush right into the Holiest of Holies, but had restrained himself.

As the day wore on his companions were increasingly downcast, frustration showing itself in quick tempers and petty irritations. How much they wanted Thomas to believe!

But if he told them once, he told them many times, "Unless I see the—"

They hushed him with a wave of the hand and he smiled at them kindly, knowing they would eventually come to realize they were mistaken. A full week had passed, and Thomas made up his mind he'd wait around only one more day, then he'd have to pick up the pieces and make a new life for himself.

On the eighth day they had come full-cycle, and another week had begun. All the pilgrims were gone, the marketplace was resuming its usual business, and the disciples were talking about trying to go their separate ways. They must play it safe, they said, but in a few days the situation should ease and perhaps they could slip away from the city unnoticed.

Having settled it in their minds what they planned to do, they seemed more relaxed and talkative. On that first day Thomas listened as the women compared notes with Simon Peter and John, retelling how one week before they went to the tomb, how they saw angels and all. They went into great detail, saying where the angels sat, how they sounded, what they said. To Thomas it was all the memory of a shared fantasy and, nothing more, and had it not been so tragic it would have been amusing.

Nothing Thomas said to Mary Magdalene shook her confidence that she herself had seen Jesus, that he had talked with her. Poor woman; with her history of demons it was easy to see that her mind was playing tricks on her.

Simon Peter was just as convinced as Mary Magdalene that he, too, saw and talked with Jesus. *Well, it's no wonder he's thought up this ridiculous story,* Thomas said to himself. *After what he did, he's bound to be guilt-ridden. I don't say he's wittingly lying; under that kind of guilt any man's mind would conceive a defense.*

Thomas looked around the table at the faces of the men sitting there, their wives and other women standing with arms folded, and he wondered that such sensible people had become victims of such delusion. To a man they believed that in this very room Jesus had come back and talked with them after his death. *Well,* Thomas allowed, *seeing Jesus suffer as he did is enough to bring on manifestations of nervous prostration.* He rubbed the knuckles of his left hand. *I know. I watched him die. It's enough—*

Without warning Thomas felt a tension in the room and heard a small stir. Following the stares of the others, he saw a figure standing in the middle of the floor! Quickly he glanced at the door. It was bolted shut. His heart thumping in his chest, he thought, *What is this?*

"Peace be with you!" Was it Jesus? He was coming toward Thomas, the others standing aside, making room.

Cold with fear Thomas half-rose, his eyes meeting Jesus' eyes. Speaking only to him, Jesus held out his hands and said, "Put your finger here; see my hands."

Trembling, Thomas obeyed, touching the rough scars in both his hands.

Pulling aside his garment to bare his body Jesus told him, "Reach out your hand and put it into my side."

Again Thomas obeyed, placing his palm against the warm flesh of Jesus' side. Feeling the jagged wound, Thomas thought his heart would leap out of his body.

"Stop doubting and believe," the Lord commanded him.

So weak he could not stand Thomas sank to his knees, and looking up at Jesus he found his voice. "My Lord and my God!"

"Because you have seen me, you have believed; blessed are those who have not seen and yet have believed."

# 18

# Five Hundred and More

... MOST OF WHOM ARE STILL LIVING, THOUGH SOME HAVE
FALLEN ASLEEP.

Scripture Reference: Matthew 28:16;
1 Corinthians 15:6, 7; Matthew 17:1–13

J esus told the Eleven to go to a certain mountain in Galilee and he would meet them there. They obeyed, and they were not alone, for more than five hundred of the brothers assembled there. With the mountain air filling their lungs, the wispy cloudstuff of the spring sky streaking the blue, James remembered other times when Jesus had gone up on a mountain to be alone and pray.

James was thinking about the time he, John, and Peter climbed a mountain with Jesus. What a memorable experience awaited them there! It was by far the most glorious event of all the events he had witnessed during the life of Jesus, and how difficult it had been to keep confidential what had happened that day. So many times he wanted to tell his wife, but he had kept the secret. While he reminisced it occurred to him that perhaps now—

Getting up, he sought out Simon Peter and John, and taking them by the arms he led them over to one side. "Remember the time we went up on the mountain—"

John's face brightened, "I was thinking about that very same thing!"

"He commanded us not to speak of that day," Peter cautioned. "I wouldn't—"

James was quick to interrupt. "Don't you remember? He

said we were not to speak of it until the Son of Man was raised from the dead."

John and Peter exchanged glances.

"Well?"

They both agreed. "You're right. That's what he said."

"You agree then that we can tell it now?"

They nodded their assent.

While they waited for Jesus to come James beckoned Matthew and Thomas to one side, and sitting down on the slope James began telling the story. "Do you remember that day my brother, John, Peter, and I went up on the mountain with Jesus to pray?"

They remembered.

"Well, do you remember that a few days before we went up on that mountain, Jesus told us and some Pharisees that there were some of us standing there who would not taste of death until we saw the Son of Man coming in his kingdom?"

"I remember," Matthew said.

"And I," Thomas added.

"Well, we were the privileged ones! We saw Jesus in the glory of his kingdom."

"What do you mean?"

"Up on that mountain, we saw Jesus transfigured. There was this heavenly light about him—his clothing was glistering white—

Matthew beckoned to the other disciples, "Come hear this!" Quickly they gathered around, and James repeated the description of the radiant glory of God and then told them about seeing Moses and Elijah.

"How could you recognize Moses and Elijah?" Thomas asked. "You've never seen them."

"Oh, Thomas," John said, "you would've known them. They were talking with Jesus about the death he would suffer—oh, Thomas, you would've known them!"

James and John then fell silent, reluctant to tell the rest. But Simon Peter, struggling against the embarrassment, told how he suggested to the Lord that three shrines be built, "One booth for Moses, one for Elijah, and one for Jesus—memorials, you know. Then we heard a voice coming from a cloud just above us—or was it all around us?" Peter didn't wait for an answer. "I felt rebuked by the voice speaking from that cloud. It was the same voice we heard when Jesus was baptized, and the words were almost the same as at the baptism. 'This is my Son whom I love; with him I am well pleased. Listen to him.' "

Peter was interrupted by the people's sudden excitement, and looking around they saw that Jesus was coming down the mountain above them. As he made his way toward them, a murmur was going through the crowd. Some of the people, seeing him approaching, bowed their heads and worshiped him, but others were doubting that he was Jesus. "Are you sure?" someone asked, and another said, "I can't be certain, I only saw him once before."

"I understand their doubting," Philip told the disciples. "When Jesus first appeared in the upper room I had to touch him before I could believe he was alive. Not until I felt Jesus' arm, was I convinced he was alive in the same body in which he had been buried. Give the people a few minutes—let them hear Jesus—they'll believe."

Jesus came close by where the disciples were standing and stopped. When he did a hush spread over the vast crowd as they waited for him to address them. In a loud clear voice he spoke. "All authority in heaven and on earth has been given to me."

No one challenged his claim, not a voice was raised, for the majority of the multitude believed he was the resurrected Christ, and they hung on his every word. "Therefore go and make disciples of all nations, baptizing them in the name of the Father and of the Son and of the Holy Spirit—"

James nudged his brother. "You hear that, John?"

"I hear—'Father, Son, and Holy Spirit,'—is that what you mean?"

He nodded. "One God in three persons?"

"The same and equal, James."

"But distinct."

"True."

They turned their attention back to Jesus who was saying, "Teaching them to obey everything I have commanded you. And surely I will be with you always, to the very end of the age."

James breathed easier. "It means," he told his brother, "that Jesus won't leave us."

"With Jesus along maybe we'll have the courage to do as he commands—make disciples of all nations. You and I have never been a hundred miles from home, James, and I for one have no interest in foreign places. Do you really think he means 'all nations'?"

"That's what he said, John."

When they came down from the mountain the crowd dispersed, going in all directions, telling the good news that they had seen the Lord.

It was not long afterward that someone told the disciples Jesus had visited his half-brother James. What they talked about no one knew, but the Lord's brother became a believer and wanted to be in the company of the disciples. Another of Jesus' half-brothers, Judas, was also now convinced of all Jesus' claims.

In time the disciples saw how different James and Judas were from what they had been. Before the crucifixion the brothers were anything but believers. How well the disciples remembered the time they came with Mary and wanted to take Jesus home with them because they thought he was beside himself! Worse than that, the brothers once challenged Jesus to go to Jerusalem, knowing how dangerous it would be for him there at the Feast of Tabernacles. They challenged him because they did not believe he was the Messiah.

"They're truly different now," James told the others. "Do you notice that James and Judas no longer refer to Jesus as their brother, but worship him and call him 'Lord'?"

"Well, it's no wonder they're convinced," Matthew said, "after all they've seen and heard."

Thomas looked thoughtful. "Aye, but there are those to come who will not have seen and heard, yet will believe. They, too, will be blessed."

# 19

# Breakfast By The Sea

IT IS THE LORD!

Scripture Reference: John 21; Luke 5:1–11

J ohn climbed in the boat behind James. Already the sun
was sinking behind them and as they thrust out from land,
Nathanael and Thomas pulled on the oars while Simon Peter,
stripped to the waist, handled the rigging to raise the sail.

Fishing was Simon Peter's idea and the rest of them were
going along for want of something better to do. John helped
James throw out the first net, watched it sinking, and wondered if fishing was what he'd be doing the rest of his life. As
marvelous as it was to know Jesus was alive, he was confused
as to what was expected of him and the other disciples. It was
all so different now—Jesus appearing and disappearing—
whereas before they had been together all the time, eating,
sleeping, talking. How quickly those days had passed and
now—*Well, who knows what the future holds?* he thought.

The last of the water birds was flying overhead, calling to
its mate following swiftly behind. It was John's favorite time
of day, and he thought of the many times Jesus had been in the
boat with them on this same water.

James was pulling in the net and John grabbed one side to
help. From the feel of it, he knew they had no great catch.
Pulling it on deck, he threw out the shellfish attached to the
net and threw back the little carp caught by the gills. Again
they slung the net over the side and let it drag behind the boat.

Gazing up at the stars appearing one by one, John remembered the time Jesus had borrowed Simon Peter's boat. He sat in the boat anchored just off shore and taught the people sitting on the beach. Afterward, Jesus told Peter to throw the net over the side.

John smiled at the remembrance. Peter had just washed that net and John knew he didn't want to throw it in the water because he'd have to wash it all over again. They'd been fishing all night and had caught nothing, so there was no reason to believe he'd catch anything if he tried again. But, reluctantly, Simon Peter did cast the net.

After a little while, when he tried to bring it up the net was so full Simon Peter had to call him and James to come help him. That catch of fish was one of the largest John ever remembered, and just thinking about it gave him pleasure.

As the night wore on they sailed over deep water and shallow, into every cove and inlet where they thought their prospects were good, but each time they pulled in the net it was empty. They were worried about filling orders for fish. For too long they'd neglected their business, and now it looked as if they'd have nothing to show for their night's work.

"It's not the right time of the moon," Thomas said. The others thought the fish were swimming too deep or were on the other side of the sea. John's back muscles ached from all the casting and he wished for the morning.

Taking turns with the nets, and even trying to spear the fish, the men kept trying for hours. At last they all despaired and retired to the bow of the boat where they could settle down and talk.

They were tired and sleepy, but with the events of the past few days their minds were uppermost on Jesus. They reviewed the occasions when he had been seen since his resurrection, and anticipated what he might do now that he was alive again.

The first gray streaks of dawn were showing above the hills

when the fishermen decided to head for shore. Worn out, and discouraged from having caught nothing all night long, they were ready for breakfast and a good long sleep.

Already the sea birds were about their morning flights and shortly the sky would lighten and turn a soft rosy color. John stretched his aching muscles and thought how hungry he was.

Sailing with the wind abeam they were making good time when, about a hundred yards off shore, they saw a man on the beach. He called out to them, "Friends, haven't you any fish?"

His strong voice carried over the water, and they answered back, "No."

He said, "Throw your net on the right side of the boat and you will find some."

John looked at his brother James, and the decision was clear. "What do we have to lose?" James asked. Grabbing the heavy wet net, Nathanael, Thomas, and Simon helped them heave it over the side one more time.

In a little while James gave the signal. They started pulling up the net, but discovered they were no match for the weight of it! Seeing the predicament, every man aboard lent a hand. "Never have I seen such a catch of fish!" Nathanael exclaimed.

But John remembered something and, straining to haul in the catch, he yelled, "It is the Lord!"

As soon as Peter heard that he dropped the net, grabbed his garment, and wrapped it around him. John glanced over his shoulder and saw Peter diving overboard.

"We'll have to tow the catch ashore," someone said. Lowering the sail they manned the oars.

As they rowed John watched Peter swimming until he stumbled out of the water onto the beach. Jesus had left the fire and was coming down to meet Peter.

In a little while the disciples brought the ship as far as they could and let down the anchor. As they were securing the boat the tantalizing smell of baking bread and frying fish wafted out to them.

"Bring some of the fish you have just caught," Jesus told them, and Nathanael was quick to fetch them.

Dragging the net up on the beach, James and John counted the fish—one hundred and fifty-three! Checking the net carefully, they could not find a single tear.

Jesus invited them, "Come and have breakfast."

Warming himself by the fire, the dusky rose sky reflecting in the water, John watched as Jesus took the bread and passed it to each of them, then the fish. The act was a familiar one—Jesus serving them—and, as Jesus stretched out his scarred hand to reach him, John received his portion with gratitude.

Stripping the flesh from the bones, the men ate hungrily, happy to again be in the company of their risen Lord. When they finished eating they leaned back to rest. Soon Jesus turned to Simon Peter and asked, "Simon son of John, do you truly love me more than these?"

"Yes, Lord," he answered and squirmed a bit. "You know that I love you."

Jesus said, "Feed my lambs."

Then he asked again, "Simon, son of John, do you truly love me?"

Visibly perturbed, Simon answered, "Yes, Lord, you know that I love you."

"Take care of my sheep."

Again, the third time, Jesus asked him, "Simon, son of John, do you love me?"

Peter grimaced, pained that Jesus pressed so hard. "Lord, you know all things; you know that I love you."

John felt sorry for Simon Peter. "Feed my sheep," Jesus was saying. "I tell you the truth, when you were younger you dressed yourself and went where you wanted; but when you are old you will stretch out your hands, and someone else will dress you and lead you where you do not want to go."

Simon's face clouded. John, as well as Peter, understood what Jesus meant—Simon Peter would die a martyr's death.

Jesus stood up and began walking away. "Follow me!"

The followers scrambled to their feet and went after him. Peter glanced back over his shoulder and seeing John, he asked Jesus, "Lord, what about him?"

Jesus answered, "If I want him to remain alive until I return, what is that to you? You must follow me."

This prompted a discussion among the disciples. "Did you hear that? John isn't going to die," one of them said.

John shook his head. "No, he didn't say that. Jesus only said, 'If I want him to remain alive until I return, what is that to you?' " But they weren't listening.

# 20

# The Fortieth Day

HE WAS TAKEN UP BEFORE THEIR VERY EYES . . .

Scripture Reference Acts 1:1–11; Luke 24:49–53

J esus and the Eleven were headed for Bethany, less than two miles southeast of Jerusalem. The familiar road climbed the Mount of Olives and led around a curve to the eastern slope. It was in Bethany that Jesus had raised Lazarus from the dead, and there he had attended the feast in the home of Simon the Leper. It was in Bethany that Mary, the sister of Lazarus and Martha, had anointed Jesus with incense for his burial.

"Maybe we're going to visit Mary, Martha, and Lazarus," Thaddeus said.

Nathanael shrugged his shoulders. "We'll see."

For forty days, nearly six weeks, Jesus had been appearing and disappearing, talking with the disciples about the kingdom of God. On one occasion while he was eating with them Jesus told them not to leave Jerusalem but to wait for the gift his Father promised. "For John baptized with water, but in a few days you will be baptized with the Holy Spirit."

So, that day when they were walking along, the disciples asked Jesus if he was going to restore the kingdom to Israel immediately. He told them, "It is not for you to know the times or dates the Father has set by his own authority."

Nathanael frowned. God gave Daniel dates concerning the

times and events to come in the future, but Nathanael did not
want to interrupt the Lord by asking questions.

"But you will receive power," Jesus was saying, "when the
Holy Spirit comes on you; and you will be my witnesses in
Jerusalem, and in all Judea and Samaria, and to the ends of the
earth."

Nathanael could not understand how the Holy Spirit
would enable them to do the impossible and thought to himself, *No man among us was up to witnessing in Jerusalem, not
with the opposition there. Nor in Judea, for that matter—even
Jesus could do no great work among the fierce religious sects active
in Judea. To speak of Christ there, a man's life would not be worth
a straw.*

*As for the Samaritans—! They are outcasts, how can Jewish
men talk to them?*

Nathanael, who had lived most of his life in Cana, could not
think beyond the boundaries of his own country, for he had
never been farther than Tyre and Sidon. What he had seen of
those port cities made him want never to leave his native
Galilee again. How could he be expected to go to the ends of
the earth?

When the little party reached the gentle eastern slope outside of Bethany, they stopped under a fig tree. Nathanael
sensed nothing unusual even when Jesus raised his arms and
began blessing them. But while Jesus was blessing them he was
taken up from them!

Nathanael stood aghast. He could not believe his eyes! A
cloud simply enveloped Jesus and he was lost from sight.
Nathanael's last glimpse of him was of his feet. In astonishment all the disciples were gazing after Jesus, frantic to
know what was happening. Nathanael's pulse throbbing in
his head, the blood pounding, he thought, *He's leaving us!
He's leaving us!*

Suddenly two men clothed in white garments stood among
them. "Men of Galilee," they said, "why do you stand here
looking into the sky? This same Jesus who has been taken from

you into heaven will come back in the same way you have seen him go into heaven."

"*Come back*"? Nathanael repeated to himself. *When? What do they mean, "in the same manner"? In the clouds?*

The Lord's spectacular departure happened so quickly, so silently, it left the disciples in a state of shock. And as suddenly as the visitors had appeared, they departed. Nathanael looked from one face to another, trying to determine what his friends were thinking. "Were those men in white angels?" he wondered aloud. "Who were they?"

No one answered.

The throbbing in his head was no better, but when the others finally turned to go back to Jerusalem, Nathanael followed. Whatever awaited them there was a mystery, but the promise of the Father concerned the Holy Spirit. Whatever it meant, Nathanael determined to have that promise.

As he walked along, his mind so frenzied by what had happened he could not concentrate, words of John the Baptist were coming to him over and over again. "I baptize you with water for repentance. But after me will come one who is more powerful than I, whose sandals I am not fit to carry. He will baptize you with the Holy Spirit and with fire."

Nathanael did not understand a baptism of the Holy Spirit and fire, but a sense of anticipation came over him, and the pulsation in his head quickened. "Thomas, wait up for me," he called, and ran to catch up with his friend.

# 21

# Three Thousand Enemies Believe

GOD HAS MADE THIS JESUS, WHOM YOU CRUCIFIED,
BOTH LORD AND CHRIST.

Scripture Reference: Acts 1:12–2:47

O ne hundred and twenty believers were waiting in Jerusalem in an upstairs room, waiting for the Father to send the Comforter. None of them knew precisely what they were waiting for, what manifestation they would receive of the Holy Ghost's presence; but in obedience to Jesus' command and with faith in the promise they gathered. They had been praying and waiting for ten days. During those days pilgrims had been pouring into Jerusalem from all the provinces, coming to the Temple to celebrate the Feast of Pentecost. It was a feast of thanksgiving and faith. Offering the first fruits of their harvest, they thanked God in expectation of a full harvest to come.

While the believers waited, the disciples selected Matthias by lot to take Judas Iscariot's place among them, so now they were Twelve again. After that there was little else to do but wait and pray. After the titanic experiences they had been through the ten days of isolation gave them time to reflect, time to calm down.

On that tenth morning, suddenly, there came a noise from heaven, like the sound of a violent wind filling the house! It wasn't wind, for there was no sand blowing in the window, only the sound of wind—a roaring. The sound was accompanied by what seemed to be flames of fire that separated like licking tongues, and came to rest upon the head of each of them. It was the baptism of fire! They were being filled with the Holy Spirit!

With the Holy Spirit enabling them, the whole company began speaking in languages they did not know! A great sense of confidence came over them, and given a zeal they had never known before, they piled out of the house, rushed down on the street.

Jewish pilgrims outside the house heard the commotion, saw the hundred and twenty coming down the stairs and hurried to see what was going on. Hearing the believers speaking in foreign dialects, the languages of the pilgrims, they were astonished. "Are not all these men who are speaking Galileans?" they asked, and assured that the men were native Galileans, they asked, "Then how is it that each of us hears them in his own native language? We hear them declaring the wonders of God in our own tongues!"

Confused and alarmed, they kept asking, "What does this mean?"

But there were others among them who laughed at the Spirit-filled believers. "They've had too much wine!" they said.

Simon Peter and the Eleven stood up on the steps to answer the charge. "Fellow Jews and all of you who are in Jerusalem, let me explain this to you," Peter said. "Listen carefully to what I say. These men are not drunk, as you suppose. It's only nine in the morning! No, this is what was spoken by the prophet Joel: 'In the last days, God says, I will pour out my Spirit on all people. Your sons and daughters will prophesy, your young men will see visions, your old men will dream dreams . . .'"

Thomas was also able to recall the prophecy, and for the first time understand its fulfillment. From his vantage on the stairs he could see most of the crowd, spread out as far as the city wall. Among the pilgrims in their foreign dress were members of the Sanhedrin, Pharisees, scribes, traders, soldiers—and they were plainly frightened. There were followers of John the Baptist huddled alongside the wall where the disciples stood, and women with babes in arms. Thomas recognized many men who had been at the trial accusing Jesus, and others who jeered him as he hung on the cross. *They have a right to be afraid*, he thought. Their astonishment was far different from the snarling, hateful expressions they wore that other day.

"Men of Israel, listen to this," Peter shouted. "Jesus of Nazareth was a man accredited by God to you by miracles, wonders, and signs, which God did among you through him, as you yourselves know."

Before Jesus' resurrection there would have been an outcry from many of these people; but as Thomas listened for some challenge, some heckling, there was none—not a peep.

"This man was handed over to you by God's set purpose and foreknowledge," Peter told them, "and you, with the help of wicked men, put him to death by nailing him to the cross."

Even Peter's harsh incrimination did not call forth one objection! To Thomas their silence acknowledged their guilt. All over Jerusalem people agreed that Jesus had been unjustly tried and executed, and Thomas was curious to know how those who persecuted Jesus were reacting. There were several antagonists whom he remembered from the crucifixion standing near, and he watched their faces to see if there was any sign of repentance. One of them bore an agonizing countenance; another man's mouth twitched with nervousness; and some could not hold up their heads.

Peter, speaking in the power of the Holy Spirit, continued. "But God raised him from the dead freeing him from the agony of death, because it was impossible for death to keep its hold on him."

Not even the Sadducees raised a voice to deny that God had raised Jesus from the dead. Thomas told himself that if anyone in that crowd could have produced the corpse of Jesus, he would have done so. But not one person disputed the fact that Jesus was raised from the dead. *It's public knowledge,* he said to himself. *The truth has been so verified his resurrection is accepted.*

The multitude listened intently as Peter spoke. "David said about him: 'I saw the Lord always before me. Because he is at my right hand, I will not be shaken."

Thomas recognized the Psalm and quoted it under his breath with Peter. "Therefore my heart is glad and my tongue rejoices; my body also will live in hope, because you will not abandon me to the grave, nor will you let your Holy One see decay."

The Holy Spirit began revealing the meaning of the words to Thomas . . . David was writing a prediction of Jesus' resurrection. . . . God, unwilling for the Lord's body to decay, had raised him from the dead on the third day before decay set in.

"God has raised this Jesus to life," Peter said, "and we are all witnesses of the fact."

Thomas smiled. Simon Peter was not the same man. Six weeks before he was wildly whacking off a man's ear trying to defend Jesus, then later swearing he didn't know Jesus. There was no explaining the change in Peter, his understanding and his boldness, except to say he was given the power of the Holy Spirit.

Peter's voice boomed. "Exalted to the right hand of God, he has received from the Father the promised Holy Spirit and has poured out what you now see and hear."

Thomas watched a Sadducee pressing his palms against his ears to shut out the truth.

"For David did not ascend to heaven," Peter was saying, "yet he said, 'The Lord said to my Lord: Sit at my right hand until I make your enemies a footstool for your feet.' "

He paused then thundered, "Therefore let all Israel be assured of this: God has made this Jesus, whom you crucified, both Lord and Christ."

The rapt attention of the people suddenly broke, and they clamored for help from Peter and the other apostles. "Brothers, what shall we do?" they pleaded.

Peter replied, "Repent and be baptized, every one of you, in the name of Jesus Christ so that your sins may be forgiven. And you will receive the gift of the Holy Spirit. The promise is for you and your children and for all who are far off—for all whom the Lord our God will call."

Peter kept talking, warning them, compassionately pleading with them. "Save yourselves from this corrupt generation."

They began to come, acknowledging their sins, confessing Jesus of Nazareth as Messiah and Lord. Thomas saw the Sadducee turn and run the other way—and there were others who left the scene. But of the multitude three thousand of them repented of their sins and asked to be baptized in the name of Jesus Christ. Among them were the very villains who had crucified him!

Matthew touched his arm. "Come along, Thomas. We must prepare for the baptisms."

"Matthew, do you see what I see? In the faces of our friends, in the faces of the women—Mary Magdalene and the others—all those who were in the room waiting?"

"Noticed what, Thomas?"

" . . . I don't know how to say it—but there is something of the radiance of God about them."

"Yes, Thomas, you say it well. Our risen Lord has turned our sorrow into joy unspeakable and full of glory."

# CHRISTIAN HERALD
## People Making A Difference

Christian Herald is a family of dedicated, Christ-centered ministries that reaches out to deprived children in need, and to homeless men who are lost in alcoholism and drug addiction. Christian Herald also offers the finest in family and evangelical literature through its book clubs and publishes a popular, dynamic magazine for today's Christians.

## Our Ministries

**Family Bookshelf** and **Christian Bookshelf** provide a wide selection of inspirational reading and Christian literature written by best-selling authors. All books are recommended by an Advisory Board of distinguished writers and editors.

**Christian Herald magazine** is contemporary, a dynamic publication that addresses the vital concerns of today's Christian. Each monthly issue contains a sharing of true personal stories written by people who have found in Christ the strength to make a difference in the world around them.

**Christian Herald Children.** The door of God's grace opens wide to give impoverished youngsters a breath of fresh air, away from the evils of the streets. Every summer, hundreds of youngsters are welcomed at the Christian Herald Mont Lawn Camp located in the Poconos at Bushkill, Pennsylvania. Year-round assistance is also provided, including teen programs, tutoring in reading and writing, family counseling, career guidance and college scholarship programs.

**The Bowery Mission.** Located in New York City, the Bowery Mission offers hope and Gospel strength to the downtrodden and homeless. Here, the men of Skid Row are fed, clothed, ministered to. Many voluntarily enter a 6-month discipleship program of spiritual guidance, nutrition therapy and Bible study.

**Our Father's House.** Located in rural Pennsylvania, Our Father's House is a discipleship and job training center. Alcoholics and drug addicts are given an opportunity to recover, away from the temptations of city streets.

Christian Herald ministries, founded in 1878, are supported by the voluntary contributions of individuals and by legacies and bequests. Contributions are tax deductible. Checks should be made out to Christian Herald Children, The Bowery Mission, or to Christian Herald Association.

Administrative Office: 40 Overlook Drive, Chappaqua, New York 10514
Telephone: (914) 769-9000

Fully-accredited Member
of the Evangelical Council
for Financial Accountability